W9-DBH-316

The Skeletal and Muscular Systems

THE HUMAN BODY
How It Works

THE HUMAN BODY
How It Works

The Skeletal and Muscular Systems

Gregory J. Stewart, Ph.D.

INTRODUCTION BY

Denton A. Cooley, M.D.

President and Surgeon-in-Chief
of the Texas Heart Institute
Clinical Professor of Surgery at the
University of Texas Medical School, Houston, Texas

CHELSEA HOUSE
PUBLISHERS
An imprint of Infobase Publishing

THE SKELETAL AND MUSCULAR SYSTEMS
Copyright © 2009 by Infobase Publishing

Chelsea House
An imprint of Infobase Publishing
132 West 31st Street
New York NY 10001

Library of Congress Cataloging-in-Publication Data

Stewart, Gregory J.
The skeletal and muscular systems / Gregory J. Stewart.
p. cm. — (The human body: how it works)
Includes bibliographical references and index.
ISBN 978-1-60413-365-3 (hardcover)
1. Musculoskeletal system—Juvenile literature. I. Title. II. Series.
QM100.S74 2009
611'.7—dc22   2008052560

Chelsea House books are available at special discounts when purchased in bulk
quantities for businesses, associations, institutions, or sales promotions. Please call
our Special Sales Department in New York at (212) 967-8800 or (800) 322-8755.

You can find Chelsea House on the World Wide Web at
http://www.chelseahouse.com

Series design by Erika Arroyo, Erik Lindstrom
Cover design by Takeshi Takahashi

Printed in the United States of America

Bang EJB 10 9 8 7 6 5 4 3 2 1

This book is printed on acid-free paper.

All links and Web addresses were checked and verified to be correct at the time of
publication. Because of the dynamic nature of the Web, some addresses and links may
have changed since publication and may no longer be valid.

Contents

Introduction

THE HUMAN BODY IS AN INCREDIBLY COMPLEX AND amazing structure. At best, it is a source of strength, beauty, and wonder. We can compare the healthy body to a well-designed machine whose parts work smoothly together. We can also compare it to a symphony orchestra in which each instrument has a different part to play. When all of the musicians play together, they produce beautiful music.

From a purely physical standpoint, our bodies are made mainly of water. We are also made of many minerals, including calcium, phosphorous, potassium, sulfur, sodium, chlorine, magnesium, and iron. In order of size, the elements of the body are organized into cells, tissues, and organs. Related organs are combined into systems, including the musculoskeletal, cardiovascular, nervous, respiratory, gastrointestinal, endocrine, and reproductive systems.

Our cells and tissues are constantly wearing out and being replaced without our even knowing it. In fact, much of the time, we take the body for granted. When it is working properly, we tend to ignore it. Although the heart beats about 100,000 times per day and we breathe more than 10 million times per year, we do not normally think about these things. When something goes wrong, however, our bodies tell us through pain and other symptoms. In fact, pain is a very effective alarm system that lets us know the body needs attention. If the pain does not go away, we may need to see a doctor. Even without medical help, the body has an amazing ability to heal itself. If we cut ourselves, the blood-clotting system works to seal the cut right away, and the immune defense system sends out special blood cells that are programmed to heal the area.

During the past 50 years, doctors have gained the ability to repair or replace almost every part of the body. In my own field of cardiovascular surgery, we are able to open the heart and repair its valves, arteries, chambers, and connections. In many cases, these repairs can be done through a tiny "keyhole" incision that speeds up patient recovery and leaves hardly any scar. If the entire heart is diseased, we can replace it altogether, either with a donor heart or with a mechanical device. In the future, the use of mechanical hearts will probably be common in patients who would otherwise die of heart disease.

Until the mid-twentieth century, infections and contagious diseases related to viruses and bacteria were the most common causes of death. Even a simple scratch could become infected and lead to death from "blood poisoning." After penicillin and other antibiotics became available in the 1930s and 1940s, doctors were able to treat blood poisoning, tuberculosis, pneumonia, and many other bacterial diseases. Also, the introduction of modern vaccines allowed us to prevent childhood illnesses, smallpox, polio, flu, and other contagions that used to kill or cripple thousands.

Today, plagues such as the "Spanish flu" epidemic of 1918–19, which killed 20 to 40 million people worldwide, are unknown except in history books. Now that these diseases can be avoided, people are living long enough to have long-term (chronic) conditions such as cancer, heart failure, diabetes, and arthritis. Because chronic diseases tend to involve many organ systems or even the whole body, they cannot always be cured with surgery. These days, researchers are doing a lot of work at the cellular level, trying to find the underlying causes of chronic illnesses. Scientists recently finished mapping the human genome, which is a set of coded "instructions" programmed into our cells. Each cell contains 3 billion "letters" of this code. By showing how the body is made, the human genome will help researchers prevent and treat disease at its source, within the cells themselves.

The body's long-term health depends on many factors, called risk factors. Some risk factors, including our age, sex, and family history of certain diseases, are beyond our control. Other important risk factors include our lifestyle, behavior, and environment. Our modern lifestyle offers many advantages but is not always good for our bodies. In western Europe and the United States, we tend to be stressed, overweight, and out of shape. Many of us have unhealthy habits such as smoking cigarettes, abusing alcohol, or using drugs. Our air, water, and food often contain hazardous chemicals and industrial waste products. Fortunately, we can do something about most of these risk factors. At any age, the most important things we can do for our bodies are to eat right, exercise regularly, get enough sleep, and refuse to smoke, overuse alcohol, or use addictive drugs. We can also help clean up our environment. These simple steps will lower our chances of getting cancer, heart disease, or other serious disorders.

These days, thanks to the Internet and other forms of media coverage, people are more aware of health-related matters. The average person knows more about the human body than ever before. Patients want to understand their medical conditions and treatment options. They want to play a more active role, along with their doctors, in making medical decisions and in taking care of their own health.

I encourage you to learn as much as you can about your body and to treat your body well. These things may not seem too important to you now, while you are young, but the habits and behaviors that you practice today will affect your physical well-being for the rest of your life. The present book series, YOUR BODY: HOW IT WORKS, is an excellent introduction to human biology and anatomy. I hope that it will awaken within you a lifelong interest in these subjects.

Denton A. Cooley, M.D.
President and Surgeon-in-Chief
of the Texas Heart Institute
Clinical Professor of Surgery at the
University of Texas Medical School, Houston, Texas

1

The Skeletal and Muscular Systems

Anyone who has ever observed a "strongman" competition, in which the competitors perform feats of strength such as balancing a metal beam across their knees and supporting thousands of pounds of weight on their lower legs, has probably marveled at what seems like an impossible feat. Similarly, anyone who has been to a professional ballet performance might watch in awe as the lead dancer, in performing a series of leaps and turns, appears to defy gravity. Strength competitors and dancers may appear to perform the impossible. However, the skeletomuscular system, a combination of the body's skeletal system and muscular system, is responsible for these acts of strength, power, and grace. We will see that what at first appears impossible is probably better described as difficult but possible (Figure 1.1).

The secret to the heavy weight–balancing act is not extra muscle in the competitors' bodies, but actually the incredible strength of the bones of the legs. By balancing the weight directly over the long line of the bones of the lower legs, and by not attempting to move the weight once in place, the "strongman" or "strongwoman" can support weights many times greater than his or her weight. As we will see, the ability to support extraordinary weight is an important feature of many of the bones of the body. The secret to the dancer who appears to defy gravity lies in the incredible strength of the muscles of the

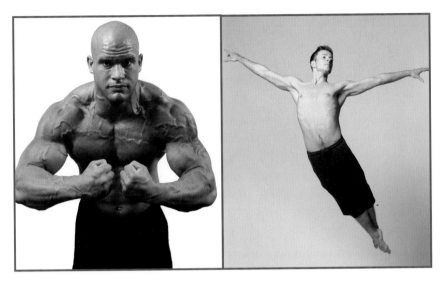

Figure 1.1 The skeletomuscular system is responsible for both the strength and grace of our movements. The bodybuilder (*left*) illustrates the strength our bodies can achieve. The ballet dancer (*right*) demonstrates the grace and precision of movement we can achieve.

legs. The dancer has strengthened and trained the muscles of the legs to propel him or her high off the stage and to complete graceful turns and twists before landing. These are dramatic examples of the power and precision of the skeletomuscular system, but the everyday movements that our bones and muscles allow each of us to perform are no less amazing. As we move through this book, we will discover the importance of our skeleton and muscles and how these combined systems contribute to our ability to function from day to day.

THE SKELETAL AND MUSCULAR SYSTEMS WORK TOGETHER

Although bones and muscles each have other important functions, they primarily work together to move the parts of the body. Muscle is the only tissue in the body that has the ability to contract, or shorten, so all body movements involve muscle of some kind. The kind of muscle that works with the bones of the skeletal system is called **skeletal muscle**, and unlike other kinds of muscle, it is under voluntary control—we can make it contract at will.

Muscle can contract, but unless it has something to pull against, it cannot move a body part. The body moves when muscles attached to bones pull on the bones, thereby moving part of the body. Both ends of skeletal muscles are attached to bones. By contracting between two bones, the muscles change the position of those bones relative to each other, which causes the body to move. Generally, one bone basically remains stationary, while the other moves. In Figure 1.2, when the biceps muscle contracts, the lower arm is pulled upward while the upper arm remains stationary. A simple way to envision this is to take two pieces of wood that are joined with a hinge. If you put hooks in the free ends of the pieces of wood and

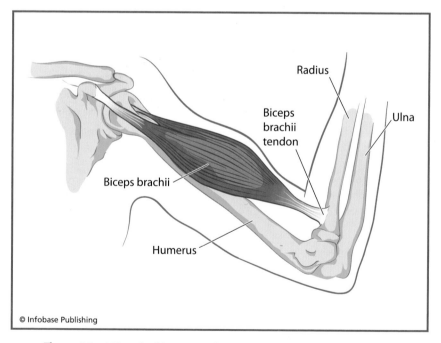

Figure 1.2 When the biceps muscle contracts, or shortens, it pulls on the radius of the forearm, which flexes the arm at the elbow.

attach a rubber band to them, the two pieces of wood will snap together. If you stretch the rubber band without attaching it to the hooks, it simply goes back to its original shape without moving anything but itself. For muscles to do work, they must be attached to bones.

Skeletal muscles must work in **opposing pairs** for normal body function. As we will see later in this book, skeletal muscles work only by pulling on bones. They cannot push on them. As a result, skeletal muscles must work in pairs to provide a full range of movement for a particular bone or **joint**—a point where two bones come together. (The joint in Figure 1.2 is the elbow joint.) Thus, while contraction of the biceps moves the lower arm up, when the biceps relaxes, another muscle must contract to pull the lower arm down. Together the two muscles are an opposing pair, moving the lower arm in two directions.

CONNECTIONS

The skeletal and muscular systems work together to form a closely integrated system. The skeletal and muscular systems each have a number of critical functions. For some of these functions, the two systems are dependent on each other, while other functions, are unique to a specific system. As we proceed through this book, we will learn more details about the components of the skeletomuscular system and will explore the common and the unique characteristics and functions of these components. Using the bones and muscles of your hands and arms, turn the page and begin your exploration of the "movers and shakers" of the human body.

2

Bones and Other Skeletal Components

THE HUMAN SKELETON IS LOCATED INSIDE THE BODY TISSUES, and therefore is called an **endoskeleton**. Other animals, such as insects and crustaceans (shellfish), have an **exoskeleton**—a rigid, tough, outer protective layer that covers their soft tissues. Exoskeletons, which are found only in some invertebrates, provide strength and a degree of movement, but they have their limitations. For one thing, the growth of the animal is restricted and happens in phases. After a certain amount of growth, the exoskeleton becomes constrictive and the organism must **molt**, or shed, its exoskeleton in order to become larger (Figure 2.1). During the molting phase, these animals are particularly vulnerable to damage and to predators. Ultimately, animals with exoskeletons are limited in size, so there are no animals with exoskeletons among the largest animals on Earth or in its waters. Finally, not all organisms have skeletons. Bacteria, protozoa, and fungi are mostly microscopic single-celled organisms. Although there are structures within their cells that serve some of the functions of skeletons, these organisms do not have skeletons in the same sense as animals. As organisms become more complex and increase in size, they develop the need for a skeleton of some type.

Figure 2.1   Insects are encased in a hard shell, or exoskeleton. As the insect grows, this exoskeleton becomes so confining that it must be shed. A new, larger exoskeleton forms after the old one is completely shed.

COMPOSITION OF BONE TISSUE

Bone contains both organic and inorganic substances. The organic parts of bone include living cells—the **osteoblasts** and **osteoclasts**; **ground substance**, which consists of **glycoproteins** (proteins modified with sugars) and **proteoglycans** (sugars modified with **amino acids**); and collagen. The remainder of bone (about 65%) is composed of inorganic salts, mainly calcium phosphate. The organic components, particularly the collagen, account for the resilience of bone (its ability to resist breaking when stressed), while the inorganic components account for its hardness.

Bone is a dynamic structure—it is constantly changing. Osteoblasts are cells that build new bone tissue, while osteoclasts are cells that break down bone. This allows bone to grow, heal, and adapt to changing conditions.

STRUCTURE OF BONES

A bone appears, at first glance, to be a solid structure, like a rock. But living bone is actually a complex network of channels and solid sections (Figure 2.2). A thin section of bone examined under the microscope shows these channels. Each channel has two parts. The outer portion is a series of concentric rings that form the **osteon**. The osteon is shaped like a cylinder and runs parallel to the long axis of the bone. The opening in the center of the osteon is called the **Haversian canal**. Blood vessels and nerves pass through the Haversian canals.

The structure of the osteon makes bone strong. The layers of the concentric rings consist of long **collagen fibers** composed of tough connective tissue. These fibers are arranged in a helix, or spiral, rather than in a straight line. They curve around the central axis of the canal like a spring. This spiral structure contributes to the strength of the osteon, and is further strengthened by the fact that each individual layer of the concentric rings spirals in the direction opposite the layers on either side of it. By alternating the direction of the collagen

THE FATE OF A SOFT-SHELL CRAB

Crabs are marine (ocean-dwelling) animals that have exoskeletons. When a crab grows, it gets bigger and bigger until its rigid exoskeleton will not let it grow any further. At this point, the crab sheds its exoskeleton and makes a larger one, allowing the crab to continue to grow. In the Chesapeake Bay area of Maryland, the region's famous soft-shell crabs shed their exoskeletons around May of each year. Immediately after they shed their tough coats, the crabs are extremely vulnerable to predators, particularly to people who make a living fishing for them. Because the tough outer layer is missing, the entire crab is edible. No mallets or cracking tools are needed to enjoy a delicious feast of soft-shell crabs. You simply cook them, then pop them in your mouth and chew.

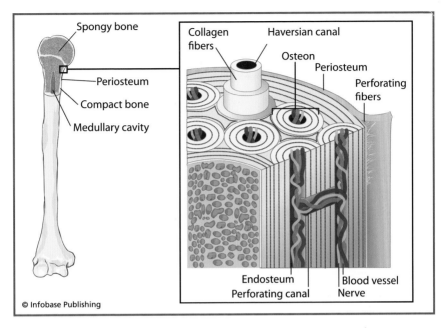

© Infobase Publishing

Figure 2.2 Although bones are extremely sturdy structures, they are not completely solid. There are small openings containing cells, small canals running between the trapped cells, and larger channels through the bone that contain blood vessels and nerves.

spirals, the osteon becomes extremely strong. A closer look at the bone section under the microscope reveals another group of channels that moves away from the Haversian canals at right angles. These are the **Volkmann's (perforating) canals**. These canals contain blood vessels and nerves that enter the bone from the periosteum.

The Periosteum

The **periosteum** is a double membrane that surrounds the outside of a bone (*peri* means "around" and *osteum* means "bone"). The membranous coat of the periosteum consists of two layers. The tough, fibrous outermost layer serves as a protective coating. The inner layer, called the **osteogenic layer**, is responsible for the growth and reshaping of bones. (*Osteo* means "bone," and *genic* means "to make or create.") Two basic types of cells are found within this layer: **osteoblasts**, or bone-building cells, and **osteoclasts**, or bone-destroying cells. An easy way to remember these cells is that "osteoBlasts Build," while "osteoClasts Crunch" (destroy) bones. The periosteum is anchored to the bone itself by bits of collagen called **Sharpey's perforating fibers**.

The Endosteum

Long bones have a hollow core. This core is lined by another membrane, called the **endosteum** (*endo* means "inside" and *osteum* means "bone"). This membrane also lines the canals of the bone. Like the periosteum, the endosteum contains osteoblasts and osteoclasts, which allow bone to grow from the inside as well as the outside.

FUNCTIONS OF BONES

Bones are the foundation on which the rest of the body is built. As a result, they are the first components that define our shape and form. Bones also serve a number of specific functions that may not be obvious. It is important to remember that not all bones serve the same function. Each bone is specialized for its location and the job it must perform. Even bones on the right side of the body are slightly different from the same bones on the left side of the body, as they have mirror-image curvature rather than identical curvature.

The first basic function for the skeletal system and its bones is support. Bones serve as a framework to which the other organs and tissues of the body are attached. If you have ever seen a contractor building a house, you may have noticed that the frame is the first thing to go up after the foundation is laid. It is the framework that supports the house, divides it into rooms, and to which the outside walls, the inside walls, the floor, the ceiling, and the electrical and plumbing components are attached. The frame of a house is very sturdy. If constructed properly, the house can withstand tremendous forces and remain intact. So, too, the framework of your skeleton provides the strength for your body. In order to meet the demands of this function, the bones must be strong. The bones of the legs must hold the weight of the entire body, and when we run or jump, we increase the force on the leg bones many times over. The rib cage must hold the weight of the chest away from the lungs and heart so they can function. The bones of the arms, working with the muscles, allow us to pick up items much heavier than our arms themselves. These are only a few examples of how the bones provide support.

The second primary function of the bones is protection. Bones act as an armor of sorts. In this case, the armor is covered with a layer of skin and muscle, but certain bones are protective nonetheless. The bones of the cranium, a part of the skull, protect the soft tissue of the brain, the control center for the body. The vertebrae surround and protect the **spinal cord**, the main communication cable between the brain and the rest of the body. If either of these organs is damaged, the body either ceases to function or may be permanently impaired. The rib cage protects the lungs and heart from damage from outside the body, and the bones of the **pelvis** cradle the internal organs and, in pregnant women, the developing fetus.

The third function for the bones is movement. Although the muscles are critical for movement, they must have a solid structure to work against. The ends of skeletal muscles are attached to bones. The bones then act as levers, magnifying the power of the muscles and allowing specific parts of the body to move. The muscles of the legs would not allow us to walk were they not attached to the bones of the pelvis, legs, and feet. Likewise, the muscles of our hands and arms would not make ordered and powerful movements were they not attached to the shoulders, arms, and hands. Even the process of breathing would not be possible were it not for the spinal column, the ribs, and the sternum. Both the muscles and the bones are essential for the graceful movements our bodies make.

The fourth function of the bones is the formation of blood cells. Blood cells are formed from special cells in the bone marrow—the soft center of many bones. In a process called **hematopoiesis**, these **bone marrow stem cells** give rise to all of the critical cells of the blood. Defects in the bone marrow can cause serious problems. For example, if too many white blood cells are produced, a form of cancer called **leukemia** results. If not enough red blood cells are made, a condition called **anemia** results. Not surprisingly, the activity of the bone marrow stem cells is carefully regulated. Without enough red blood cells, or **erythrocytes**, the transport of oxygen from the lungs to the body tissues is decreased, as is the transport of carbon dioxide from the body tissues to the lungs. Without enough white blood cells, or **leukocytes**, the immune system cannot protect the body properly. The synthesis of blood cells is an often overlooked but vital function of the bones of the skeleton.

The fifth function of bones is to serve as a reservoir for minerals. Bones contain high concentrations of the elements calcium and phosphorus. Both of these elements are essential. Without enough calcium and phosphorus in the diet, the needed minerals will be removed, or leached, from the bones. This causes the bones to weaken, which can lead to deformity or breakage. You may have heard that women need more calcium than men. This is generally true because women lose significant amounts of calcium during menstruation. This calcium must be replaced. As we age, our bodies become less efficient at incorporating calcium and phosphorus (in the form of phosphate) into the bones, with the result that the bones become weaker and more brittle. Older individuals are often "stooped"; that is, their shoulders roll forward and their backs curve. This is due to loss of calcium and phosphate, which weakens the bones, allowing them to deform. Calcium is also essential for muscle strength, and as the muscles become weaker, the weight of the head tends to tilt the neck and shoulders forward. Exercise is the best way to avoid stooping. It not only strengthens the muscles, but also promotes incorporation of calcium and phosphate into the bones. You may also have heard that older people are more likely to fracture their hips. The hips are the center point where the weight of the body is concentrated. As the bones of the pelvis lose calcium and phosphorus, they become more brittle and are more prone to break. Hip fractures are particularly difficult to heal because of the constant stress that is applied to the pelvis by the weight of the body. For this reason, hip fractures are very serious injuries for the elderly, and many older adults never fully recover from a broken or fractured hip.

The final function of the bones we will discuss is communication. The tiny bones of the inner ear transmit vibrations from the **tympanic membrane**, or eardrum, to other structures of the ear, which stimulate nerve impulses that reach the part of the brain that processes sound. Without these three tiny bones, we would not be able to hear. Likewise, the skeleton plays an important role in our ability to speak. A special type of cartilage, the **respiratory cartilage**, forms the **larynx**, or **voice box**, which allows us to generate the vibrations that eventually become sounds and words. The role of soft skeletal tissues is discussed in Chapter 5.

TYPES OF BONES

The 206 bones of the human body are classified according to their shape. The four major classes of bones are long bones, short bones, flat bones, and irregular bones (Figure 2.3).

Long bones are much longer than they are wide. The central portion of a long bone, called the **shaft**, is surrounded by the **ends**. The shaft of a bone is also called the **diaphysis**, and the ends are called the **epiphyses** (singular, *epiphysis*). All the bones of the legs except the **kneecaps** and **ankle bones** are long bones, and all the bones of the arms except the **wrist bones** are long bones. The name "long bones" can be misleading. Many of the long bones, including those of the hands and feet, are actually quite small. The term *long* refers to their relative shape, not their size.

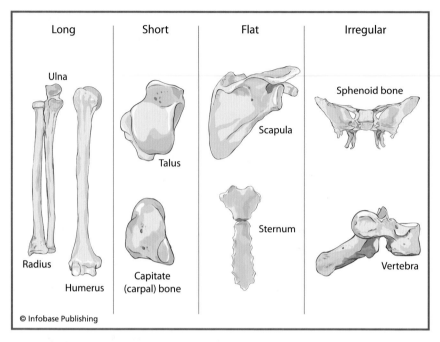

Long | Short | Flat | Irregular

Ulna

Radius

Humerus

Talus

Capitate
(carpal) bone

Scapula

Sternum

Sphenoid bone

Vertebra

© Infobase Publishing

Figure 2.3   There are four major kinds of bones in the human skeleton based on shape: long, short, flat, and irregular. Each type of bone gets its name from its general shape.

By contrast, **short bones**, such as those found in the wrist and ankle, are nearly as long as they are wide and thick. This gives the bones an almost cubelike shape, like the shape of dice. One special group of short bones is the **sesamoid bones**. These bones usually have one rounded end and a more pointed end. Their shape is similar to sesame seeds, thus the name "sesamoid." The **patella**, or kneecap, is an example of a sesamoid bone.

The third group of bones is the **flat bones**. Flat bones tend to be wider than they are thick. Flat bones include the **sternum**, or breastbone; the **scapulae** (singular, *scapula*) or shoulder blades; the **ribs**—the series of bones that protect the chest cavity; and most of the **skull**—the bones that make up the head and jaw.

The final class of bones includes those that do not fit neatly into one of the other three categories. These are called

irregular bones. Among the irregular bones are the **hip bones**; the **vertebrae** (singular, *vertebra*), the bones that form the backbone; and the bones of the inner ear.

THE BONES WILL TELL

In ancient times, fortune tellers would take the bones of an animal (usually a sheep), mix them, and toss them out of a bag to form a pattern, in the manner of throwing dice. The fortune tellers believed they could predict or "divine" the future based on the patterns that the bones formed, a practice called astragalomancy. Although there is no evidence that this practice was effective, modern scientists have learned that the bones of crime victims can sometimes reveal facts about the crimes. **Forensic science** involves studying evidence from a crime scene to learn more about the crime and what happened to the victim.

Forensic anthropologists study the bones of dead people to determine what they can about the victim. What kinds of things can a forensic anthropologist find out? Based on the bones alone, these scientists can determine the age, race, sex, and relative size of the victim. In some cases, they can accomplish this with only one or just a few of the 206 bones of the human body. Based on the mineral composition of the bones, the scientist can tell whether the victim died from certain types of poisons. The forensic anthropologist can use X-ray records to confirm whether a victim matches the X-rays of known missing persons (this is even possible using only dental X-rays). The bones can indicate if the person was a victim of repeated physical abuse, and can provide useful information about the diet of the victim. Finally, if a source of DNA is available from a suspected victim or her or his relatives, DNA can be extracted from the victim's bones and sequenced, allowing a definitive match of the bones to a particular person.

Analysis of bones to solve crimes has become a fascinating subject in detective fiction. If you are interested in this topic, you can read about the work of fictional scientists Dr. Kay Scarpetta in the books of author Patricia Cornwell, or of Dr. Temperance Brennan in the novels of Kathy Riechs.

CONNECTIONS

In this chapter we have learned that bones come in a variety of shapes and sizes and that each bone contributes to the function of the part of the body where it is located. We have learned that bones play a number of roles in the body. They provide a framework and protection, work with muscles for movement of body parts, produce blood cells, and store minerals. We have seen that bone is more than a solid, rigid rod. It is a network of canals surrounded by layers of collagen and calcium phosphate. This network of canals is critical for bone growth and change. We have also seen that bone cells are specialized, including cells that build up the bone matrix and those that remove it. The action of these cells makes bone dynamic and constantly changing. In the next chapter, we will look at the two divisions of the skeleton.

3

The Axial Skeleton

THE DIVERSITY OF ALL 206 BONES OF THE HUMAN SKELETON make it a challenge to study. Fortunately, the body has developed in such a way that there are **lines of symmetry**—imaginary lines that can be drawn through the skeleton so that the parts of the skeleton on either side of the line are mirror images, or near mirror images, of each other. The most important line of symmetry is the **medial line**, or midline, an imaginary line that runs from the center of the skull, through the trunk of the body, and directly between the legs (Figure 3.1). It is a line that divides the body into left and right sides. Thus, the medial line runs along the center axis of the body. Unless a birth defect or an injury has altered one or both sides, the right arm is a mirror image of the left arm, and the right leg is a mirror image of the left leg.

For ease of description, the skeleton is divided into two sections: the axial skeleton and the appendicular skeleton. The **axial skeleton** includes the skull, vertebral (spinal) column, and the bony thorax, which surrounds the chest cavity. This structure consists of the thoracic vertebrae, the ribs, and the sternum (breastbone). While the bones of the axial skeleton vary greatly in their appearance, the primary function of all of them is to prevent damage to the delicate central nervous system, the lungs, and the heart.

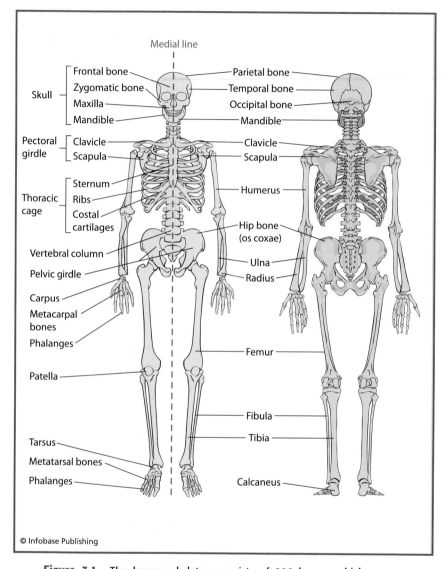

Figure 3.1 The human skeleton consists of 206 bones, which are organized along lines of symmetry for the body. At left, an anterior view of the human skeleton, and right, a posterior view.

The bones of the body that are not part of the axial skeleton are part of the **appendicular skeleton**. The word *appendicular* comes from the same root as *appendix*, meaning "an

TABLE 3.1

SKELETON	STRUCTURE	BONES
Axial skeleton	Skull	Cranium
		Nasal bone
		Maxilla
		Mandible
	Vertebral column	Cervical vertebrae (7)
		Thoracic vertebrae (12)
		Lumbar vertebrae (5)
		Sacrum (fused) (5)
		Coccyx (fused) (4)
	Bony thorax	Sternum
		Xiphoid process
		Thoracic vertebrae
		Ribs
	Pectoral girdle	Clavicle
		Scapula
	Upper Limb	Humerus
		Radius
		Ulna
		Carpals (8)
		Metacarpals (5)
		Phalanges (14)
Appendicular skeleton	Pelvic girdle (fused)	Ilium
		Ischium
		Pubis
	Lower limb	Femur
		Tibia
		Fibula
		Tarsals (7)
		Metatarsals (5)
		Phalanges (14)

appendage" or "something added on." The appendicular skeleton includes the bones of the arms and legs and the bones needed to attach those structures to the axial skeleton. In this chapter, we will explore the bones of the axial skeleton (Figure 3.2), and the bones of the appendicular skeleton will be the focus of Chapter 4. The goal of these chapters is not to memorize each bone of the body, but rather to understand how certain bones or groups of bones work together for a specific purpose. You can always refer to a textbook for the names and locations of different bones. Here, we will focus on the form and function of bones and bone groups.

THE SKULL

The skull consists of the bones of the head (Figure 3.3). We can further divide these bones into two major groups: the cranium and the mandible. The **cranium** is made up of the bones that surround the brain. The brain is the most complex organ of the body. It is the "central processor" for every other organ in our body and is composed of soft tissues. Because of its central importance in body function, the brain must be carefully protected. The bones of the cranium serve as a "helm"—the section of a knight's armor that protects the head.

The cranium can be divided into two functional groups: the vault and the base. The word *vault* brings to mind a highly protected safe or chamber. This is an apt description of the **cranial vault**. It is used to store and protect the most valuable treasure of the body: the brain. The cranial vault makes up the top, sides, and back of the skull. The other section of the cranium is the **cranial base**, which consists of the bottom of the skull. When the vault and the base are joined, they create a chamber, the **cranial cavity**. It is within this highly secure **cavity** that the brain resides, protected on all sides from possible damage.

The cranial vault is made up of eight platelike bones that curve out slightly in the middle. These bony plates meet at lines called sutures. In newborns, these sutures are not connected. This allows the bones of the cranial vault to move relative to each

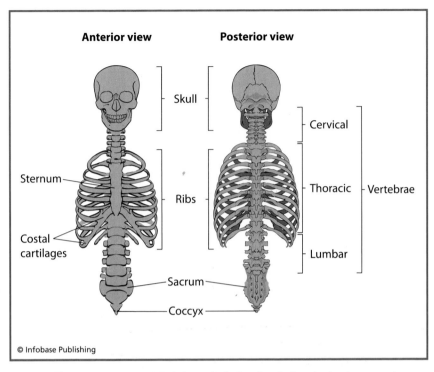

Anterior view   **Posterior view**

Skull

Cervical

Sternum

Thoracic — Vertebrae

Ribs

Costal
cartilages

Lumbar

Sacrum

Coccyx

© Infobase Publishing

Figure 3.2   The axial skeleton includes the skull, spinal column, and ribs. The primary function of the axial skeleton is to protect the brain, spinal cord, heart, and lungs.

other. This room for movement is important when the baby is born because it gives the skull flexibility as it passes through the birth canal. A newborn baby's skull is sometimes elongated or otherwise misshapen immediately after birth, but can be gently massaged and shaped to realign the bones of the cranial vault into their normal positions. Because the bones of the cranial vault will continue to grow for several years, the bones may not completely enclose the brain. You have probably been told that you must be very careful with the head of an infant because there are gaps or "soft spots" between the bones. A blow to one of these spots could result in permanent damage to the brain. The cranial base is divided by internal ridges that form three steps, or fossae (singular, *fossa*), that hold the brain snugly in place.

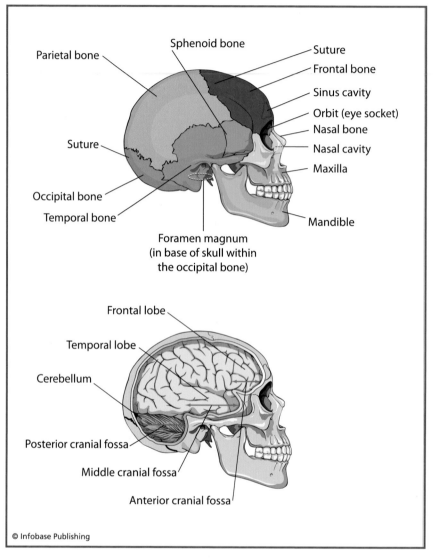

Figure 3.3   The skull, or cranium, has two major components: the vault and the base. The vault surrounds and protects the brain and consists of a series of flat bones that join together. The base consists of the point at which the spinal cord is continuous with the brain.

The cranial chamber is not the only cavity in the skull. There are cavities on either side of the skull for the middle and inner ears, and two **orbits** on either side of the front of the skull that house the eyes. Below the orbits is the nasal cavity, which is critical for the sense of smell and for respiration. There are also many other openings in the skull. These are known by a number of names, including **foramina**, or holes (singular, *foramen*); **canals**, or narrow tubes or channels; and **fissures**, or crevasses or gorges. An opening in the base of the cranium, the **foramen magnum**, serves as the point of entry for the spinal cord, and there are small cavities in the skull that accommodate the **sinuses**, small air-filled pockets that connect to the respiratory system.

The bones of the face are considered part of the skull. The **nasal bone** is found at the top of the nose where it joins the skull. If you take your thumb and forefinger, place them on either side of the tip of your nose, and wiggle gently, you will probably notice that there is considerable flexibility. This portion of the nose does not contain hard bone, but a softer, flexible skeletal tissue called **cartilage**. Cartilage does not contain a high concentration of calcium phosphate. If you now gently slide your thumb and forefinger up the sides of the nose you will feel a slight ridge. If you wiggle your thumb and finger above this ridge you will notice that it is very rigid. This is the hard nasal bone. On either side of the nasal bone is the **maxilla**. The maxilla extends down and around from the nasal bone, encircling the nasal cavity, and serves as the anchor site for the upper row of teeth. Attached below the cranium, on the front side, is the **mandible**, or jawbone. If you move your jaw, you will see that it moves up and down, and wiggles side to side. The mandible joins to the cranium at two points on each side. These points are rounded and attached in such a way as to allow a wide range of motion, which enables us to chew our food and form sounds for speech. The mandible is the strongest bone of the face. Starting at the chin, the mandible is relatively flat as you move backward on both sides. Somewhere in a line below the ear, the bone angles upward to ultimately come in close contact with the cranium. If you run your fingers along the jaw from the chin backward, you can probably feel this angle. The mandible is the bone into which the lower teeth are anchored. While we have a high degree of rotation around the contact points between the mandible and cranium, we cannot completely disconnect these contacts. Many snakes can completely disconnect the mandible from the cranium, which allows them to swallow prey that is actually wider than their mouths. If you see a snake shortly after feeding, you may see a large "lump" partway down the body. This lump, the ingested prey, illustrates how disconnecting the mandible assists feeding in animals that swallow their food whole.

THE VERTEBRAL COLUMN

The **vertebral column**, which is also called the backbone or spinal column, surrounds and protects the **spinal cord** (Figure 3.4). You might think that the best protection would be provided by a structure that was a hollow cylinder, like a piece of pipe, but the vertebral column requires a high degree of flexibility. If you stand and bend at the waist, you will notice that your back curves as you bend forward. Straightening again, notice that your hips and shoulders are probably aligned. However, if you place your hands on your shoulders and twist your shoulders, you will see that the body twists beginning at the hips and continues twisting to the shoulders. Finally, if you straighten again and place your hands on your shoulders with your elbows pointing outward, you can drop your left elbow toward your feet and your right elbow will point upward. These movements show us that there is much flexibility in the vertebral column. It can bend, rotate, and shift from side to side.

This high degree of flexibility of the vertebral column is a result of its many bones. At birth there are 33 bones in the vertebral column. These bones, the vertebrae, are cylinders that form a collar around a porous core called the **vertebral body**, or **centrum** (Figure 3.4b). Extending away from most of these collars are projections of bone called **pedicles** and **processes**. In the center of each vertebra is a hole called the **vertebral foramen**,

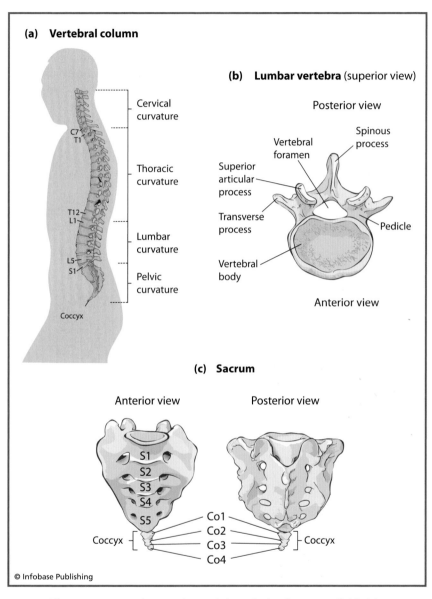

(a) Vertebral column

(b) Lumbar vertebra (superior view)

Posterior view

Cervical
curvature

C7
T1

Thoracic
curvature

T12
L1

Lumbar
curvature

L5
S1

Pelvic
curvature

Coccyx

Spinous
process

Vertebral
foramen

Superior
articular
process

Transverse
process

Vertebral
body

Pedicle

Anterior view

(c) Sacrum

Anterior view   Posterior view

S1
S2
S3
S4
S5

Coccyx

Co1
Co2
Co3
Co4

Coccyx

© Infobase Publishing

Figure 3.4   (a) The vertebrae of the spinal column are divided into groups based on where the curves of the spinal column change direction. These groups are the cervical, thoracic, lumbar, and pelvic curvatures. (b) A typical lumbar vertebra. (c) The sacrum and coccyx are located on the end of the spinal column farthest from the skull. With age, they form a spearhead-shaped mass of fused bone.

through which the spinal cord passes toward the brain. The pedicles and processes are areas of contact between vertebrae and the attachments of muscles and ligaments. **Ligaments** are connective tissues that attach bone to bone.

THE FUSED VERTEBRAE

You will recall that there are 33 separate vertebrae in the spinal column of a newborn infant. As we age, some of these vertebrae change. The four vertebrae at the bottom of the spinal column fuse together to form the **coccyx**, or tailbone (Figure 3.4c). The vertebrae that make up the coccyx are

YOUR HEALTH—SPINAL CORD INJURIES

The spinal cord serves as the main communication cable between the brain and the rest of the body. Nerves enter and leave the spinal cord at different positions along its length. Like other nervous tissues, the spinal cord cannot repair itself. Damage at any place along the spinal cord blocks the flow of messages between the brain and the parts of the body below the injured point. Thus, spinal cord injuries usually affect parts of the body below the injured site.

The two most common types of spinal cord injuries result in either **paraplegia**, a condition that allows movement of the arms and upper body, but not the lower body; or **quadriplegia**, the paralysis of all four limbs of the body. Quadriplegia will be discussed later in this chapter. Paraplegia usually occurs when a person suffers a severe, forceful blow across the upper back, or between the last of the cervical vertebrae and the first thoracic vertebrae. This can happen in automobile accidents or falls in which the person lands on his or her back. An example of the latter might be a fall from a horse or a backward fall while rock climbing. Damage to the spinal cord usually occurs somewhere within the thoracic vertebrae. This leaves the nerves of the head, arms, and upper chest unaffected, but will usually "disconnect" the nerves from the lower trunk and smaller and simpler than other vertebrae and are free of processes and pedicles. While the coccyx is generally thought to be a **vestigial structure**—that is, a structure no longer important to human function—in other animals, it is the base for the tail. The tail is often an important structure for balance; in some animals it is prehensile, which means that it can be used for grasping and holding. In these animals, the bones of the tail are not fused. Occasionally, babies will be born with an unusually long coccyx, resulting in a short "tail" extending from the base of the spine. Physicians usually remove this tail shortly after birth.

legs from the brain. The result is that the paraplegic generally is able to breathe normally and use the arms, head, and neck, but has no control over the legs and may have difficulty or a complete inability to control bladder and bowel functions. Paraplegics can usually live very productive lives, although they are most often confined to a wheelchair.

Many paraplegic accidents can be avoided if you are careful. Being a cautious driver and paying close attention to what you and others are doing will reduce the risk of paraplegia from an automobile accident. This is why it is so important to concentrate your total attention on driving when you are behind the wheel of a car. Avoid distractions such as cell phones and passengers who take your attention away from the road. Many automobile accidents can be prevented if you remember that the only focus for your attention when you are behind the wheel is driving—nothing else matters. Accidents such as those that are the result of falls from horseback riding or rock climbing are best avoided by being well trained in what you do. These athletic activities require special equipment and knowledge, and should not be attempted without proper preparation. The majority of paraplegic events that result from sports happen to inexperienced participants.

Above the coccyx are another five vertebrae that fuse as we mature. These form the **sacrum** (Figure 3.4c). The sacrum is shaped like a spearhead that points downward. Not only are the collars fused, but the processes and pedicles are also reshaped and fused to form nearly flat panels with four holes in each side panel. The sacrum is the point of attachment for the hips.

QUADRIPLEGIA

Quadriplegia is a condition in which all four limbs are paralyzed. It is a more life-threatening condition than paraplegia because it affects the vital function of breathing. Many quadriplegics need mechanical assistance to breathe properly. Additionally, use of a wheelchair is more difficult because a quadriplegic does not have use of the arms. In most cases, quadriplegia occurs when a severe blow is delivered directly to the skull. If the blow is delivered from the side, the sudden force may cause one or more cervical verte-brae to damage or sever the spinal cord. A blow from the front or the back can force the cervical vertebrae to pinch or cut the spinal cord. As a result, a quadriplegic may be left with control of only the head and perhaps some of the neck muscles. Mechanical wheelchairs are now available that can be directed with a stream of breath from the mouth, or by a machine that monitors the move-ment of the eyes.

One of the most common ways that people can fall victim to quadriplegia is swimming accidents—more specifically, diving accidents. If a person dives into water that is too shallow, or is shallower than she or he anticipated, the person's head will hit the bottom of the pool or pond with tremendous force. This may immediately sever or damage the spinal cord, or it may fracture one of the cervical vertebrae. Diving accident victims must be carefully removed from the water, avoiding movement of the head or neck region, because a fractured vertebra may damage the spinal cord further even after the initial injury has occurred. This is why lifesav-ers move very cautiously when they remove a diving accident victim from the water. Usually, they will first carefully tie the victim onto a backboard to provide support for the neck and back, and to prevent

THE UNFUSED VERTEBRAE

Moving up from the coccyx to the top of the sacrum, the vertebrae gradually get larger. Above the sacrum are the vertebrae that are unfused in most individuals. As you move up toward the skull, these vertebrae gradually get smaller. We will discuss these vertebrae from top to bottom, moving from the skull toward the sacrum.

movement of the head. These precautions reduce the likelihood of secondary injury.

Why do diving accidents tend to cause quadriplegia more often than paraplegia? The most important factor is that the cervical vertebrae are smaller and weaker than the thoracic or lumbar vertebrae. As a result, they are more delicate and prone to damage, especially from a blow to the head. You can avoid these injuries by never diving in shallow water and never diving into water if you do not know the bottom conditions or its depth.

One other common cause of quadriplegia (as well as paraplegia) is motorcycle accidents. Unlike a car, a motorcycle provides little protection for its rider. Quadriplegic accidents can be significantly reduced, however, by simply wearing an approved motorcycle helmet. The helmet helps keep the head aligned with the body, which reduces strain on the cervical vertebrae and protects the brain from injury in the event of a crash. The most common cause of adult-acquired epilepsy (a condition that results in uncontrollable seizures of the body) is motorcycle accidents in which the rider was not wearing a helmet.

The purpose of this section is not to discourage you from swimming, driving, or riding a motorcycle. Rather, the goal is to emphasize the importance of proper training, practice, and use of the correct equipment, as well as undistracted focus on the task at hand. Paying close attention to possible risks will not only make for a more exciting and enjoyable experience, but may preserve your ability to live your life to the fullest in the future. You are your own best defense against spinal cord injuries. Though some cases are unavoidable, many can be prevented or minimized with proper care, training, and attention.

The unfused vertebrae can be divided into three major groups. While the number of vertebrae in each group varies in 5% of the population, generally we have the same number of vertebrae in each group. How do we divide these vertebrae into groups? In a healthy person, the spinal cord is not straight, but curves (Figure 3.4a). It actually changes direction at two points, dividing the vertebrae into three sections. The top section, always consisting of seven vertebrae, curves forward toward the chest. These vertebrae are called the **cervical vertebrae** and the concave curve is called the **cervical curvature**. The seven vertebrae, starting at the skull end, are called the C1 through C7 vertebrae. These are the smallest, lightest, and weakest of the vertebrae. Vertebrae C1 and C2 are different from the others, since they are the contact point with the skull and form the first vertebral joint.

The second group of vertebrae usually consists of 12 vertebrae. These are the **thoracic vertebrae**, which curve toward the back. As you move down these vertebrae from T1 at the top to T12 at the bottom, the vertebrae increase in size, weight, and strength. The thoracic vertebrae are the points where the ribs attach to the spinal column in the back of the body.

The third set of vertebrae, the **lumbar vertebrae**, usually consists of five vertebrae. These continue to enlarge as you move downward from L1 to L5. Like the cervical section, the curvature of the lumbar regions is toward the front, or belly. The projections of these vertebrae restrict rotation more than the cervical and thoracic vertebrae, providing a strong support for the base of the spinal cord.

One way to remember how many vertebrae form each section of the spine is to associate each with a typical mealtime. If you eat breakfast around 7 A.M., lunch around 12 noon, and an early dinner around 5 P.M., you can remember the cervical (7), thoracic (12), and lumbar (5) vertebrae. The fused vertebrae can be remembered by "f," for "fused." There are five fused vertebrae in the sacrum and four fused vertebrae in the coccyx.

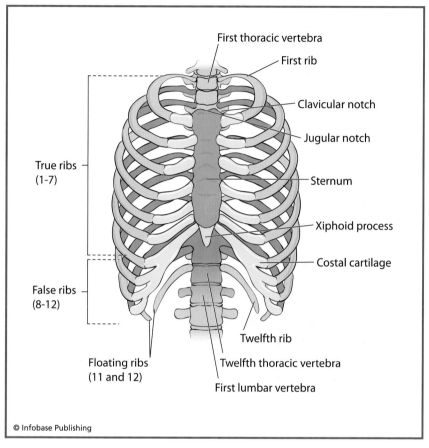

First thoracic vertebra

First rib

Clavicular notch

Jugular notch

True ribs
(1-7)

Sternum

Xiphoid process

Costal cartilage

False ribs
(8-12)

Twelfth rib

Floating ribs
(11 and 12)

Twelfth thoracic vertebra

First lumbar vertebra

© Infobase Publishing

Figure 3.5   The bony thorax consists of the spinal column, the ribs, and the bones of the breastplate. Together they form a strong cage that both protects the heart and lungs and helps drive the breathing process.

THE BONY THORAX

The **bony thorax** is a cage of bone that surrounds the chest cavity (Figure 3.5). It consists of the sternum, or breastbone, the 12 thoracic vertebrae, and the ribs. The sternum is a flat plate of bone in the center of the chest; it is formed by the fusion of three bones. There is an indentation at the top of the sternum, called the **jugular notch**. If you gently allow your forefingers to travel down the front of your throat you should be able to feel this notch. From the notch, the sternum widens and then narrows again, forming a heart-shaped top to the bone. It extends downward in a daggerlike shape. The sternum finally narrows to a separate, diamond-shaped flat bone called the **xiphoid process**.

The ribs are the major bony component of the bony thorax. The ribs are slightly flattened bones that curve from the spinal column around either side of the chest, and end at the sternum in the front of the body. Starting at the top of the chest, the first seven ribs on each side are called the **true ribs** because they connect directly to the sternum through short pieces of cartilage called **costal cartilage**. The next three ribs are called the **false ribs** because each of the three upper pairs is attached to the cartilage of the rib above rather than directly to the sternum. The remaining two ribs do not connect to the ribs above or to the sternum (usually ribs 11 and 12) and are called **floating ribs**. The ribs are shorter at the top and get progressively longer from rib 1 to rib 7 (all true ribs), then decrease in length from ribs 8 to 12.

CONNECTIONS

The axial skeleton can be divided into three major sections. The skull consists of the bones that protect the brain and support the teeth. The primary functions of the skull are eating, speaking, and protecting the brain. The vertebral column consists of 33 bones, with the lower nine vertebrae fused into two structures: the coccyx and the sacrum. The other vertebrae are divided into three groups of unfused bones. Beginning at the skull, the first seven vertebrae form the cervical curve, the next twelve form the thoracic curve, and the final five bones form the lumbar curve, which rests above the sacrum. The primary function of the spinal column is protection of the spinal cord, while allowing reasonable rotation in the torso. The final group of bones in the axial skeleton forms the bony thorax, a cage of bone that surrounds the chest. This structure consists of 12 pairs of ribs, each pair of which attaches to the spinal column at a different thoracic vertebra. The top seven pairs of ribs are the true ribs and join directly to the sternum in the front of the body via costal cartilage. The next three pairs of ribs, the false ribs, only connect to the costal cartilage of the rib above. The remaining two pairs of ribs are known as floating ribs, since they do not connect to the sternum at all. The primary functions of the bony thorax are to protect the heart and lungs and to facilitate breathing.

4

The Appendicular Skeleton

THE MIDLINE, OR MEDIAL LINE, DIVIDES THE BODY INTO LEFT
and right halves, which are mirror images of each other. This
symmetry is also observed in the bones that make up the arms
and hands, and the legs and feet. If you look at an arm and
compare it to a leg, they really don't look much alike. Or do
they? If you compare the structure of the bones of the arms
with those of the legs, you will find clear differences, no doubt,
but you will also find many similarities. With a few notable
exceptions, the bones of the arms and hands are very similar
to those of the legs and feet. This is even clearer if you compare
the forelimbs (arms, in humans) of a four-legged animal, like a
cat or dog, to the hindlimbs (legs, in humans). The process of
walking on two feet rather than four has allowed animals that
walk upright to undergo changes in the upper limbs that make
them useful for grasping, holding, and maneuvering, thus
accounting for the changes we see between our upper limbs
and our lower ones. In this chapter, we will study the upper
and lower limbs that are appended, or added, to the axial skeleton. These include the shoulders, arms, hands, and fingers,
and the hips, legs, feet, and toes (Figure 4.1).

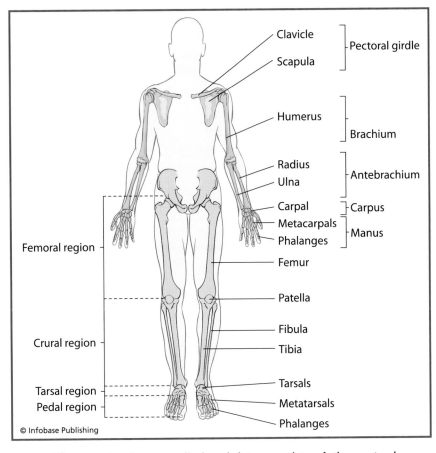

Figure 4.1 The appendicular skeleton consists of the pectoral (shoulder) girdle and the arms and hands, as well as the pelvic (hip) girdle and the legs and feet.

THE PECTORAL GIRDLE

The arms are connected to the axial skeleton at the upper region of the thoracic cavity by a series of bones collectively called the **pectoral girdle**. "Girdle" may seem like an odd name for this structure, but in this case the term refers to a structure that straddles a central axis. The pectoral girdle straddles the spinal column and upper portion of the thoracic cage. It works somewhat like a coat hanger to which the arm bones are attached. It consists of two bones on each side: the clavicle and the scapula. The innermost bone is the **clavicle**, or **collarbone**—a long, thin bone that extends across the shoulders. Because this bone is so thin, it is easily broken. A person who lifts weights or who does work that requires much upper body strength will actually have a thicker collarbone than someone who does not do such activities. Not surprisingly, thicker collarbones are less likely to get broken.

The collarbone attaches on one end to the sternum and on its other end to a **scapula** (plural, *scapulae*), or shoulder blade (Figure 4.2). The scapula is a triangular flat bone with the longer sides of the triangle angling down the back and the shorter side parallel with the top of the shoulder. As viewed from the back, the scapula has three surfaces, or fossae. Each fossa serves as an attachment point for a number of muscles that not only move the scapula, but also hold it in place. Three important regions on each scapula are the **acromion**, the outermost and upward point of the shoulder where the collarbone attaches to the scapula; the **coracoid process**, a finger-like piece of bone that serves as the attachment point for the biceps and other muscles of the arms; and the **glenoid cavity**, where the upper end of the upper arm bone (the humerus) attaches.

One of the most interesting facts about the pectoral girdle and its bones is that they are connected by loosely fitting joints that allow a wide range of motion. This gives us the mobility we need for our upper limbs and provides much more mobility and range of movement than we find in the lower limbs. Although this freedom of movement is important to humans, it is essential for other primates, such as monkeys, who need very wide-ranging movement in their upper bodies to allow them to live in the tree canopy and swing from branch to branch. We will discuss these joints in more detail in Chapter 5.

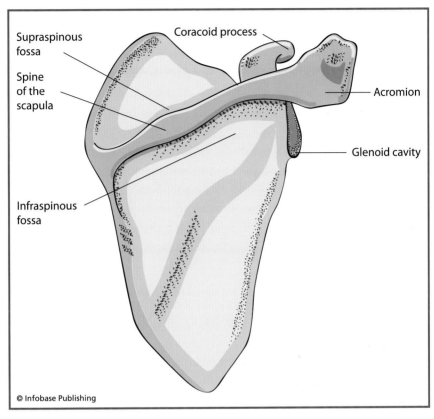

Figure 4.2 The scapula, or shoulder blade, is shaped like an irregular spearhead. In this view from the back, its parts include the coracoid process, supraspinous fossa, spine, and infraspinous fossa.

The Upper Limb

Each upper limb, or arm, in the human body consists of 30 bones. These can be divided into four groups to assist in learning their locations and functions (Figure 4.3). The upper arm, or **brachium**, extends from the shoulder to the elbow. Each upper arm has a single long bone, the **humerus**. The forearm, or **antebrachium**, extends from the elbow to the wrist. The two bones of the antebrachium are the **radius** and the **ulna**. The ulna is the slightly larger of the two bones.

The third region of the upper limb is the wrist, or **carpus**. The carpus consists of eight small bones—the **carpal bones**— arranged in a cluster that roughly forms two rows. While the humerus, radius, and ulna are all long bones, the carpal bones are short bones. The fourth region of the upper limb is the hand, or **manus**. The 19 bones of the hand can be divided into two groups. The five bones of the palm are the **metacarpals** (*meta* means "situated beyond"). You can remember that these are between the fingers and the wrists because they are the metacarpals, an extension of the carpal bones of the wrist. Thus, the metacarpals are situated beyond the carpals. The remaining 14 bones of the hand are the **phalanges** (singular, *phalanx*), the bones of the fingers and thumb.

The Humerus

The two ends of the humerus, the bone of the upper arm, are very different (Figure 4.4). The end that connects to the shoulder is a hemisphere and is called the "head." The head joins the scapula at the glenoid process. The other end of the humerus has two smooth bumps or knobs called **condyles**. One of these, the more rounded, is the **capitulum**, which makes contact with the radius. The other condyle, the **trochlea**, is shaped more like a pulley and makes contact with the ulna. The humerus flares out just above these condyles and forms two bony complexes called the **epicondyles**. One of these, the **medial epicondyle**, is called the "funny bone" because it houses the **ulnar nerve**. A sharp tap at just the right spot stimulates this nerve, which causes an intense tingling.

The Radius and Ulna

The end of the radius that attaches to the humerus is shaped like a disk and permits free rotation at this joint. This allows you to twist your palm upward or downward. The other end of the radius has three features. The **styloid process** of the radius is a projection of bone close to the thumb, the **articular facets** are indentations that interface with bones of the wrist, and the

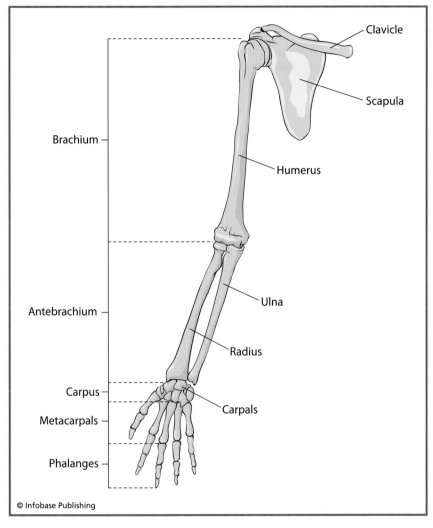

Figure 4.3 The upper right appendicular skeleton. The arm itself is made up of 30 bones.

ulnar notch is a groove where the ulna makes contact with the radius (Figure 4.5).

The ulna attaches to the trochlea of the humerus through a cup-shaped pocket called the **trochlear notch**. This joint functions like the hinge of a door, allowing the forearm to move

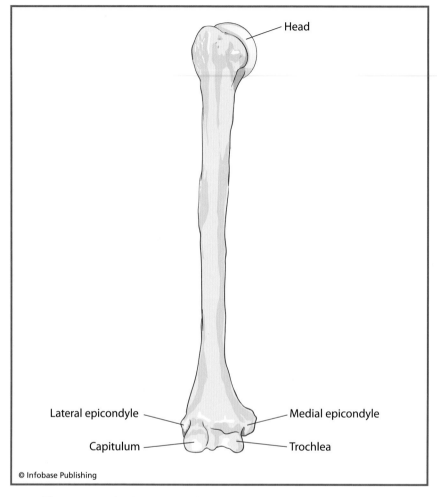

Head

Lateral epicondyle

Medial epicondyle

Capitulum

Trochlea

© Infobase Publishing

Figure 4.4   The humerus is the bone of the upper arm and is the largest bone of the upper appendicular skeleton. The ends have different structures, each fitting into a particular joint, which allows the arm to move in different directions.

at a right angle relative to the humerus. The other end of the ulna connects to the wrist through its own styloid process. If you place the thumb and forefinger of one hand at the sides of the wrist joint of the other and slide the thumb and finger up and down the wrist, the bumps you will feel are the styloid processes of the radius and ulna.

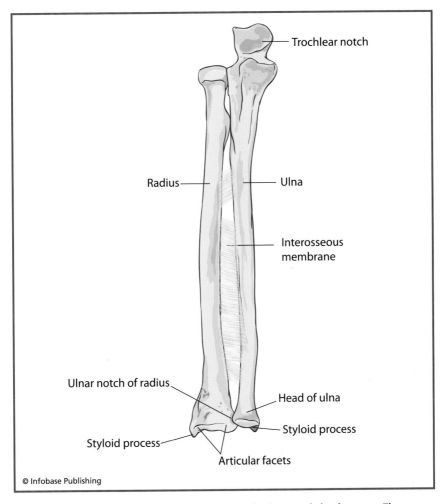

Trochlear notch

Radius

Ulna

Interosseous membrane

Ulnar notch of radius

Head of ulna

Styloid process

Styloid process

Articular facets

© Infobase Publishing

Figure 4.5   The radius and ulna are the bones of the forearm. The radius is the larger and stronger of the two, while the ulna serves as a strut, or stabilizing bone, for the radius. The radius and ulna connect to the humerus via the trochlear notch and the carpal bones of the wrist via the styloid process, articular facets, and ulnar notch.

The radius and ulna are connected to each other along their length by a special ligament called the **interosseous membrane**. This ligament allows the two bones to move over each other. This happens when you twist your wrist. Try it. Notice that not only does the wrist rotate, but also the entire forearm rotates. By having two bones rather than one in the forearm, the body can rotate one relative to the other, giving greater flexibility to the forearm and wrist.

The Carpal Bones

The eight bones that make up the wrist are arranged in two rows of four bones each (Figure 4.6). These are short bones for the most part. The first row of bones, the one closest to the elbow, contains the **scaphoid** (boat-shaped), **lunate** (moon-shaped), **triquetrum** (triangular), and **pisiform** (pea-shaped) bones. The pisiform bones are unique among the carpal bones in that they are not short bones but sesamoid bones. The four bones that make up the second row, the row closest to the hand, are the **trapezium**, an almost circular bone; the **trapezoid**, a four-sided bone with different angles; the **capitate**, the most rectangular of the bones in this row; and the **hamate**, the bone at the base of the little finger. A little hook of bone on the finger end of the hamate, called the **hamulus**, is a characteristic of this bone, and useful in identifying the hamate.

The Metacarpals and Phalanges

Metacarpals and phalanges are both long bones. The five bones of metacarpals are numbered using Roman numerals, beginning with the thumb (I) and ending with the little finger (V). In each case, the end of the bone closest to the wrist is called the **base**, the shaft of each metacarpal is called the **body**, and the end closest to the fingers is called the **head**. You can see the heads of your metacarpals when you make a fist; the **knuckles** that bulge out at the base of each finger are the heads of the metacarpals. If you look at an X-ray of your hand, the metacarpals look like extensions of the fingers because they form straight lines with the bones of the fingers, or phalanges.

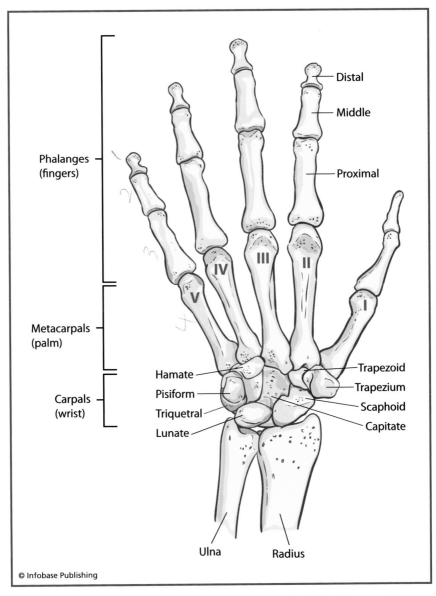

Distal

Middle

Proximal

Phalanges
(fingers)

Metacarpals
(palm)

Carpals
(wrist)

Hamate
Pisiform
Triquetral
Lunate

Trapezoid
Trapezium
Scaphoid
Capitate

Ulna   Radius

© Infobase Publishing

Figure 4.6   The hand and wrist consist of a complex fitting of extremely specialized bones. Seen here are the bones of the left wrist and hand, including the phalanges, the metacarpals, and the carpals.

There are 14 phalanges in the hand: The thumb has two phalanges (proximal and distal), and each of the four fingers, or **digits**, has three phalanges (proximal, middle, and distal). To demonstrate the difference, make a fist with your hand. The thumb bends in two sections, while each of the fingers bends in three sections. Each section is a **phalanx**. Instead of giving each phalanx a different name, we distinguish them by their position. Just as we begin numbering the metacarpals with Roman numeral I for the base of the thumb, the phalanges of the thumb are also designated with the numeral I. We also distinguish the phalanges by their relative closeness to the center of the body. The phalanx of the thumb closest to the metacarpal, and therefore closest to the center of the body, is called the *phalanx I proximal*. (*Proximal* means "closest to.") The other phalanx of the thumb would be *phalanx I distal*. (*Distal* means "farthest from.") Moving to the index finger, the phalanges would be *phalanx II proximal*, *phalanx II middle*, and *phalanx II distal*. Based on this pattern, what would you name the three phalanges of the ring finger?

THE PELVIC GIRDLE AND APPENDAGES

The pelvic girdle of an adult differs from that of an infant or young child because the bones of the pelvic girdle fuse as we get older. The two fused sections of the spinal column, the sacrum and the coccyx, form the centerline of the pelvic girdle (Figure 4.7). On either side are the **ossa coxae** (singular, *os coxae*). Collectively, these four bone complexes form a fused product that is shaped somewhat like a very shallow bowl standing on its side, with the lower rim slightly more forward (toward the front of the body) than the upper rim. The pelvic girdle serves a number of important functions: It concentrates and balances the weight of the trunk over the legs, and cradles and protects the organs of the urinary and reproductive tracts and parts of the digestive tract.

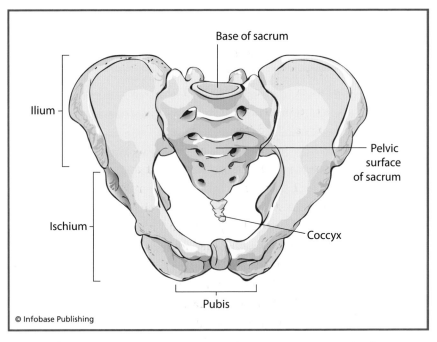

Figure 4.7 The bones of the pelvic girdle, or hips, include the ilium, sacrum, ischium, pubis, and coccyx. Through its connections to the bones of the lower body and torso, the pelvic girdle allows you to twist, turn, and swing your hips.

Each os coxae is actually created from the fusion of three bones that are separate in infants and young children. These three bones are the **ilium**, the **ischium**, and the **pubis**. The ilium is largest and is oriented toward the head. The ischium is located toward the back of the body at the bottom of the os coxae, and the pubis is located toward the front of the ischium. The pelvic girdle of a woman is generally wider and shallower than that of a man, a difference that is essential for the support of the developing fetus during pregnancy. This difference in the pelvic girdle allows forensic pathologists to determine the sex of a victim when only the skeleton remains. It also explains why women generally have wider hips, relative to the rest of the body, than men.

The Lower Limbs

Just as we were able to divide the upper limb into four sections, similarities between the bones of arms and legs allow us to do the same for the lower limbs. As we found for the upper limbs, each of the lower limbs consists of 30 bones. The four regions of the lower limb are the thigh, or **femoral region**, which extends from the hip to the kneecap; the lower leg, or **crural region**, which extends from the knee to just above the ankle; the ankle, or **tarsal region**; and the foot and toes, or the **pedal region**.

The Femoral Region

The longest bone in the body is the **femur**, the bone found in the thigh (see Figure 4.1) Not surprisingly, it is similar in shape to the humerus of the upper arm. The femur attaches to the pelvic girdle through a ball-and-socket joint. The ball is at the end of the femur closest to the hip, and the socket is created at the intersection of the ilium, the ischium, and the pubis. The femur has a long shaft that extends down the thigh, and the distal end of the femur, like the humerus, ends in two condyles.

Although not precisely a part of the femoral region, the patella, or kneecap, is usually discussed along with the femur. The patella is a sesamoid bone that is triangular in shape. It forms within the tendon of the knee, the joint between the upper and lower leg, only after we begin walking. The patella is important in both protecting and strengthening the knee.

The Crural Region

Just as there are two main bones in the forearm, there are two bones in the lower leg—the **tibia** and **fibula** (see Figure 4.1). The tibia is the larger and stronger of these two bones. It is critical for weight bearing. The fibula is a thinner bone that serves as a lateral strut. A strut is used to stabilize a structure, and the fibula stabilizes the ankle. The fibula is not designed to bear weight and would snap if the weight on the leg were not directed to the tibia.

The Tarsal Region

The bones of the ankle are similar to those of the wrist in that they are short bones that are clustered in proximal and distal groups (Figure 4.8). They differ considerably in appearance and size, however, because the ankle must support the weight of the body, while the wrists are not required to do this on a regular basis. The largest bone of the ankle is the **calcaneus**, or heel bone. The Achilles tendon joins the calf muscles to the calcaneus. If this tendon becomes cut or damaged, that leg can no longer bear weight, rendering it essentially useless. Adjacent to the calcaneus bone is the **talus**. The third bone in the proximal row is the **navicular**. The distal row of bones in the ankle consists of four bones. The largest of these is the **cuboid**. The others are the lateral, intermediate, and medial **cuneiforms**.

The Metatarsals and Phalanges

The bones of the soles of the feet are metatarsals (Figure 4.8). Like the metacarpals of the hands, each foot contains five metatarsals. These are numbered with Roman numerals as well, beginning with the metatarsal of the big toe and ending with the little toe. Metatarsals and phalanges are all long bones. Metatarsals I, II, and III connect respectively with the medial, intermediate, and lateral cuneiforms. Metatarsals IV and V both connect with the cuboid. The big toe, also known as the **hallux**, only contains a proximal and a distal phalanx. The other four toes of each foot contain a proximal, intermediate (middle), and distal phalanx. The naming and numbering of the phalanges of the feet are identical to those of the hands.

The bones of the feet and toes are positioned so that they form arches on the sole side of the foot. The arches are held together by ligaments and are important in maintaining balance. Too much weight or constant use of the feet will stretch these ligaments and will cause a condition known as fallen arches or flat feet, which makes prolonged walking and standing uncomfortable and difficult. Good-quality shoes have

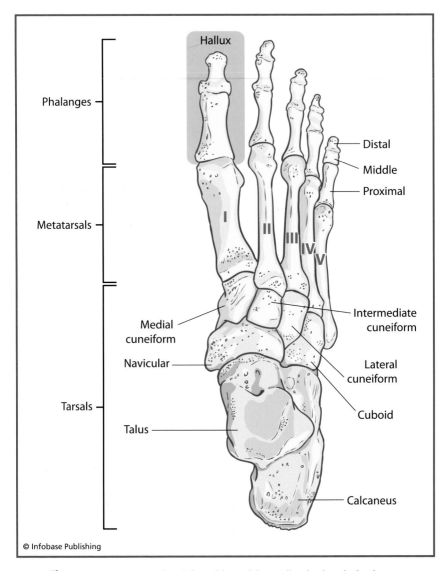

Figure 4.8   Bones of the right ankle and foot. Like the hand, the foot contains three groups of bones: the phalanges, the metatarsals, and the tarsals.

arch supports in them to take the stress off the ligaments of the feet. By wearing good-quality shoes, constant walking, running, and standing become less damaging and uncomfortable.

FOR YOUR HEALTH—BUNIONS

You may have heard of people having bunions, but do you know what they are? Although you probably think of these as problems that only affect old people, bunions can happen at any age, though they tend to get worse as we get older. A bunion is created when one of the bones of the feet shifts out of alignment, producing a protruding bump. These become irritated and can make walking difficult.

Bunions can be caused by a lot of things. They may result from an accident that damages the bones of the feet. They may be caused by arthritis, in which swelling of the soft tissue of joints forces the bones out of alignment, or from wearing shoes that do not fit properly—especially narrow or pointed shoes. Imagine that your feet are a bag of marbles. The skin and muscles make up the bag, while the bones are the marbles. As long as you do not squeeze the bag of marbles, the bag will retain its shape. However, if you put pressure on one side of the bag, or squeeze it in the middle, some of the marbles will stick out. Now imagine that you coat the marbles with superglue before putting them in the bag. If you hold the bag the same way for a length of time, the marbles will create a pattern and hold it. If this lasts long enough, the glue will set and the marbles will remain in their position even after you stop squeezing the bag. A bad pair of shoes can squeeze the bones of your feet just like the bag of marbles. If you wear the shoes long enough, the bones will remain out of alignment.

How are bunions treated? Usually, a patient goes to a specialist called a podiatrist (a doctor who treats problems of the feet). If the bunions are bad enough, the podiatrist will surgically expose the bunion to cut or shave off the protruding bone. Once the surgical site heals, the bunion no longer protrudes and does not irritate the foot anymore. However, if you continue to wear "bad" shoes, the bones of the feet will keep shifting and it may become necessary to repeat the surgery. When it comes to your feet, support and comfort are much more important than fashion. Wear "sensible shoes" and you and your feet will benefit.

CONNECTIONS

The appendicular skeleton consists of the pectoral girdle and upper limbs (arms, wrists, and hands), and pelvic girdle and lower limbs (legs, ankles, and feet). The major bones of the arms and legs and of the hands and feet consist primarily of long bones. The bones of the wrists and ankles are primarily short bones. Each upper limb and each lower limb is composed of 30 bones. There are many similarities in the composition of the bones of the upper limbs and the lower limbs; however, the demands of weight bearing have created noticeable differences in the individual bones of the upper and lower limbs.

5

Joints and Soft Tissues of the Skeleton

WE HAVE ALREADY LEARNED THAT THE SKELETAL SYSTEM is made up of bones and that these bones come together, or **articulate**, at joints. Whenever two surfaces move against each other, part of the energy expended is converted to friction, the force that works in opposition to the direction of movement. Friction can be reduced if the surfaces are lubricated. The joints of the body offer their own lubrication. This is often accomplished through soft, cushioning tissues. In this chapter, we will learn how joints allow and affect the movement of bones, and we will discover the important role that soft tissues play in protecting joints and improving their efficiency. The study of joints and their functions is called **arthrology**.

CLASSIFICATION OF JOINTS BY FREEDOM OF MOVEMENT

There are a number of ways to classify joints. One way is to consider the degree of freedom of movement at the joint. Joints like the elbow and shoulder, which have high degrees of freedom of movement, are **diarthroses** (singular, *diarthrosis*). Joints like those of the fingers and those between vertebrae, which have a more limited range of movement, are known as

amphiarthroses (singular, *amphiarthrosis*). Finally, some joints have very limited, if any, freedom of movement. Joints like the sutures between the plates of the cranium and the fused vertebrae of the lower back are known as **synarthroses** (singular, *synarthrosis*).

CLASSIFICATION OF JOINTS BY HOW THEY JOIN ADJACENT BONES

Joints can also be classified into four major categories by how they attach to adjacent bones. These categories are fibrous joints, cartilaginous joints, bony joints, and synovial joints.

Fibrous Joints

In **fibrous joints**, the collagen fibers from one bone extend and integrate into the adjacent bone. Thus, the two bones are physically joined by collagen fibers. There are three basic types of fibrous joints: sutures, gomphoses, and syndesmoses.

Sutures, which are found only in the skull, are fibrous joints that bind adjacent bones very closely and do not allow the bones to move. (Some sutures can be seen in Figure 3.3, top.) There are three types of sutures. In **serrate sutures** the connections are in the form of wavy lines, which increases the total surface of contact and makes the suture strong. In **lap sutures** the bones have beveled edges that overlap. Finally, **plane sutures** occur where two bones form straight, nonoverlapping connections.

The joints that hold teeth into their sockets are called **gomphoses**. In this case, a strong band of collagen fibers, the **periodontal ligament**, holds the tooth firmly to the jaw, but allows a little "play" so that the tooth can withstand the mechanical stress of chewing food.

The final group of fibrous joints, the **syndesmoses**, consists of joints where two bones are joined only by a ligament. These are the most flexible of the fibrous joints. The interosseous membrane, the fibrous membrane that binds the radius to the ulna and the tibia to the fibula, is an example of such a joint.

Figure 5.1 Cartilaginous joints are formed when two bones are joined by cartilage. Cartilaginous joints include synchondroses (e.g., the joints between the ribs and sternum) and symphyses (e.g., the joints between vertebrae).

Cartilaginous Joints

When two bones are joined together by cartilage, the resulting joint is called a **cartilaginous joint** (Figure 5.1). The two types of cartilaginous joints are **synchondroses**, which are joined by **hyaline cartilage**, and **symphyses**, which are joined by **fibrocartilage**. An example of a synchondrosis is the joint between the ribs and the sternum. The joint between fused vertebrae is an example of a symphysis. In this case, each vertebra is covered with hyaline cartilage, but collagen fiber bundles connect the different vertebrae together. Each connection has limited movement, but, collectively, these intervertebral discs make the spine flexible.

Bony Joints

Bony joints, or **synostoses**, result where two bones that were previously independent fuse together. This often happens as a normal part of aging. The process involves the gradual accumulation of calcium in fibrous or cartilaginous tissue through the process of **ossification**, the natural process of bone formation. Ossification occurs between the epiphyses and diaphyses of the long bones as we mature. Synostoses also occur at other junctions between bones, including the bones of the jaw and the bones of the pubic arch, a curvature of the pelvic girdle.

Synovial Joints

A **synovial joint** (Figure 5.2) is a freely movable joint in which the adjacent bones are separated by a lubricating, cushioning liquid called **synovial fluid**. Joints that do a great deal of work, including the elbows and knees, the hips, and the jaw, are often synovial joints. The synovial fluid does not freely move in and out of these joints. Instead, it is contained in a special fibrous capsule, the **joint capsule**, which creates a saclike pad filled with thick synovial fluid surrounding the joint. The ends of the bones at the joint are coated with a fibrous membrane made of hyaline cartilage and are contained within the joint capsule. The thick synovial fluid continually bathes the joint and makes the motion of the two bones relative to each other basically free of friction. In addition to lubrication, the synovial fluid acts as a shock absorber to reduce the effects of pressure on the joint.

Different kinds of synovial joints are characterized by their structure (Figure 5.3). In a **ball-and-socket joint**, the end of one bone is rounded while the end of the other bone forms a cup into which the ball fits. These joints are similar in design to a computer joystick or mouse trackball, in that they have a high degree of freedom of rotation and make the joint very versatile in its range of movement. The shoulder joint and the hip joint

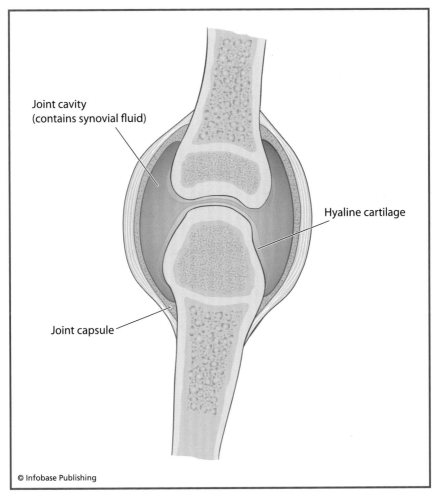

Joint cavity
(contains synovial fluid)

Hyaline cartilage

Joint capsule

© Infobase Publishing

Figure 5.2 Cross-section of a synovial joint in which synovial fluid helps to cushion the bones from impact. Examples of synovial joints include ball-and-socket, hinge, pivot, gliding, saddle, and condyloid joints.

are the two examples of ball-and-socket joints in the human body. These joints move in many directions and, as a result, they are called **multiaxial joints**.

A **biaxial joint** lets the bones move in two planes relative to each other. There are two main types of biaxial joints. The

Figure 5.3   Different types of synovial joints include ball-and-socket joints, which allow bones to move in many directions, and hinge joints, gliding joints, and pivot joints, which allow bones to move in only one direction. Saddle and condyloid joints allow bones to move in two directions.

saddle joint, found only in the base of the thumb, allows the thumb to move up and down as well as toward and away from the other fingers. Because of the range of movement at this joint, the thumb can be brought over to contact the tips of the other fingers. This feature, called an *opposable thumb*, is only found in primates (humans, apes, and monkeys). A second type of biaxial joint is found at the base of the fingers, where the metacarpals and phalanges meet. These joints, which allow the fingers to move back and forth as well as up and down, are called **condyloid joints**.

The third general group of synovial joints consists of the **monaxial joints**. These joints allow movement in only one plane or direction. **Hinge joints**, like those found in the elbow, the knee, and the fingers and toes, are all monaxial because they have only one range of motion. Another example of a monaxial joint is the **gliding joint**. In this case, the ends of the bones slide over each other, which allows for limited movement in one direction. The final example of a monaxial joint is the **pivot joint**. In these joints, a projection from one bone fits into a ring of ligament on the other. The upper two joints of the spinal column are examples of pivot joints. One allows you to move your head side to side, while the second joint allows you to move it forward and back. We also find pivot joints where the ulna and radius meet in the forearm, and where the tibia and fibula overlap in the lower leg. These joints allow you to roll one bone relative to the other. In the arm, this results in being able to turn the palm up or down, and in the leg it allows the foot to angle in or out.

Though there are many other things we could discuss about the movement of joints, we will end our discussion on joint movement here. We will conclude the chapter by describing the different types of soft tissues associated with the skeleton.

CLASSIFICATION OF SOFT TISSUES OF THE SKELETAL SYSTEM

There are three basic types of soft tissues associated with the skeletomuscular system. One type, which was previously described, provides padding to the joint. These saclike pads contain synovial fluid and are similar to shock absorbers. A pad that is positioned between bones is known as a **meniscus**.

SPARE PARTS

Like any mechanical part, the joints and bones of the skeletal system can wear out. In some cases, a joint or bone may be injured beyond repair due to an accident. In other cases, disease may cause damage to bones or joints. Finally, as medicine has become more effective, we have begun to live longer. That means that some of our joints may wear out before we do. Orthopedic surgery allows specialists to replace damaged bones and joints. In some cases, bone transplants can be performed. Generally, this involves taking a healthy bone from an organ donor and using it to replace the damaged bone in another person. This technique is growing in popularity, but as with all organ donations, we need more people to volunteer to be organ donors. Your bones do not help you after you die, but they can be recycled and may give another person a new chance for life or for better quality of life. Being an organ donor is a wonderful way to help people in need. If you are not a designated organ donor, you may want to discuss becoming one with your parent or guardian. As with blood donation, most states require that you be 18 years of age or have parental approval, be in generally good health, and have a health history that is compatible with organ/blood donation.

In transplant cases that do not use donated bones, artificial joints or bones are used to replace those that are damaged or worn out. Knee and hip replacement surgeries are common now, particularly among older individuals. The joints used are often made of stainless steel, a material the body considers "neutral" and generally will not reject. Replacement of a damaged joint with an artificial one may restore mobility to the injured patient. Recently, scientists have begun to explore the possibility of using strong, high-impact plastics as alternatives to stainless steel joints. These materials are lighter and may lead to faster healing.

Compare your body to a car. When a part of the car wears out, you replace it with a new or used one. The same thing can be done when your bones or joints wear out. Replacement of these worn-out parts restores the damaged area and leaves you ready to rev your engine and go!

We find these fluid-filled pads in the jaw and knees, among other places. Sacs of synovial fluid that are positioned between muscles or where tendons pass over bone are called **bursa** (singular, *bursae*). Specialized bursae that wrap around tendons are called **tendon sheaths**.

The second basic soft tissue of the body is the **tendon**. A tendon is a sheet or strip of tough collagen-containing connective tissue that attaches muscles to bones. The third type of soft tissue is the ligament. Ligaments are similar in structure and function to tendons, except they are used to attach bones to bones. Tendons are important for the interaction of muscles and bones, and ligaments are important in the stable association and working of a joint.

CONNECTIONS

In this chapter, we have learned that the skeleton is more than just bones. Bones articulate with each other in different ways to form joints with particular functions and ranges of motion. We have learned that joints can be classified by their mechanical design or by their range of motion and that these two methods of classification often overlap. We have also learned that soft tissues of the skeletal system—synovial pads, tendons, and ligaments—are essential for proper functioning of the skeletomuscular system.

6

Bone Growth and Repair

IN THE PREVIOUS CHAPTERS, WE DISCUSSED THE FOUR TYPES of bones and the arrangement of bones in the human skeleton. In this chapter, we consider the characteristics of bone and how bones grow and how they repair themselves. Bone tissue, or **osseous tissue**, is a specialized connective tissue. **Connective tissue** functions mainly to bind and support other tissues. Osseous tissue is hardened by the addition of calcium phosphate through a process known as **mineralization**. While osseous tissue gives bone its characteristics of strength and hardness, there are also other types of tissues in bones. Osseous tissue containing a high proportion of calcium phosphate is called **compact bone**, or dense bone, and is organized in cylinders that run parallel with the longest dimension of the bone. Compact bone is common in the shafts of weight-bearing bones, such as the long bones, and on the surfaces of other types of bones. The cylindrical arrangement of the tissue contributes to the strength of the bone.

Running the length of the shaft, or central section, of a long bone is a space called the **medullary cavity**, which contains bone marrow. The ends of the long bone contain a different osseous tissue called **spongy bone**, bone with many spaces for marrow. Though spongy bone is found in the ends of long bones, it occurs in the middle of all other types of bones. Since the spongy tissue is weaker than the harder bone of the shaft, a protective layer of compact bone always surrounds the spongy bone on the ends of long bones.

There is a trade-off in having very hard bones. The harder a substance is, the more likely it is to fracture under a sudden, strong blow. This is due to the inability of compact bone to absorb the energy of the blow. The flat bones of the skull are made in a sandwich-like fashion. They have inner and outer layers of compact bone, with a layer of spongy bone, called **diploë**, in the middle. The spaces in the spongy bone allow the energy of a blow to the head to be absorbed. While the outer layer of compact bone may fracture, only a tremendously hard blow would have sufficient energy to work through the spaces of the spongy bone and fracture the inner compact bone layer. The diploë layer thus acts as a shock absorber.

SECTIONS OF A LONG BONE

As noted previously, the shaft of a long bone is also called the diaphysis, and on either end of the diaphysis, the bone swells outward to form an epiphysis. Enlargement of the epiphysis adds strength to the joint, where much of the stress occurs in the skeletal system. The epiphysis is also the place where ligaments and tendons attach. The diaphysis provides leverage, increasing the power or the range of the muscle movements (Figure 6.1).

An *articulation* is a point where two bones come together to make a joint. At this point, the surface that forms the joint is covered by a type of hyaline cartilage called **articular cartilage**. This cartilage works with the lubricating fluids of the joint to reduce friction and to increase the efficiency of movement at the joint.

As discussed previously, bones are covered by the periosteum, an outer sheath that consists of two layers. The outer

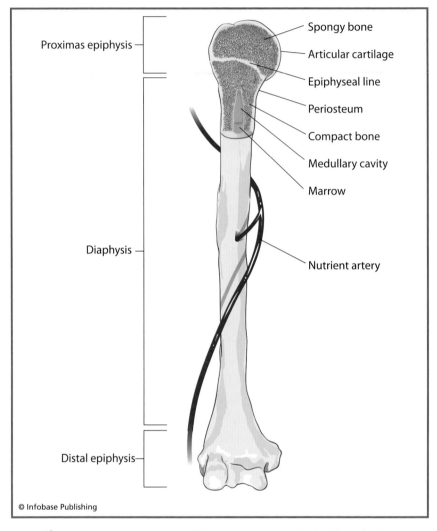

Proximas epiphysis

Spongy bone

Articular cartilage

Epiphyseal line

Periosteum

Compact bone

Medullary cavity

Marrow

Diaphysis

Nutrient artery

Distal epiphysis

© Infobase Publishing

Figure 6.1   Bones are not solid structures. Instead, they have both hollow and relatively solid portions. This structure makes them strong enough to support the body, but also provides routes for the passage of vital materials.

layer is a tough, fibrous sheet of **collagen**. The inner layer, called the *osteogenic layer* (*osteo* means "bone" and *genic* means "to create"), contains the cells that enable bone to grow, break down, and repair itself.

There is also a membrane called the *endosteum,* which lines the internal cavities of long bones. The endosteum is made of a thin layer of connective tissue that contains **osteogenic cells**, or bone-growing cells. As a result, bones grow from both the outside and the inside.

The composition of long bones changes with age. In young children, the epiphyses are separated from the diaphysis by plates of hyaline cartilage where bones grow in length. When we reach our maximum height, this plate is converted to compact bone; only a thin line remains as evidence that the cartilage plate once existed.

BONE CELLS

Like all connective tissues, bone tissue contains a mixture of ground substance, fibers, and living cells. There are four basic types of bone cells: osteogenic cells, osteoblasts, osteocytes, and osteoclasts (Figure 6.2). Osteogenic cells are found in the endosteum and in the central canals of bone. Osteogenic cells continually undergo mitosis, and some of the cells produced develop into a second type of bone cell called osteoblasts. Osteogenic cells are **stem cells**; that is, they are continually giving rise to more osteogenic cells and osteoblasts.

Osteoblasts are the cells that form bone. An osteoblast cannot undergo mitosis and, therefore, cannot reproduce. Therefore, they are produced only by conversion of osteogenic cells through a process known as **differentiation**. Osteoblasts produce the organic material found in bone and help to mineralize the bone with calcium phosphate. Osteoblasts are found in rows in the inner layer of the periosteum and in the endosteum. These cells are critical for bone growth and bone repair. Not surprisingly, stress on a bone or a bone fracture stimulate the reproduction of osteogenic cells, thus giving rise to a larger number of osteoblasts for building and repair.

The osteoblasts produce the bone matrix. Eventually they become trapped in small spaces in the matrix, at which point

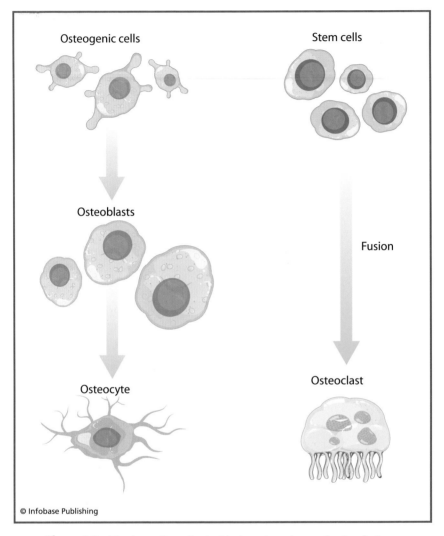

Figure 6.2   The formation of osteoblasts, osteocytes, and osteoclasts. Osteogenic cells give rise to osteoblasts, which further develop into osteocytes. Stem cells fuse to form osteoclasts.

they are called **osteocytes**, and the spaces they are trapped in are called **lacunae**. The primary role of osteocytes is to detect changes in bone and to communicate those changes to neighboring osteoblasts and osteoclasts. Tiny canals in the bone contain very thin extensions of the osteocytes and allow them to communicate with other cells. Osteocytes also assist with transferring nutrients and removing waste products from bone.

Osteoclasts are cells that remove bone. Osteoclasts are formed from bone marrow stem cells that fuse together. Thus, they are relatively large cells and have more than one nucleus, a trait common in fused cells.

Bones do not remain unchanged once they are formed. Stresses continually cause bone tissue to reform, reshape, and grow. For instance, the stress of bearing weight as we begin to walk upright signals the body to increase bone production. Lifting weights and other forms of weight-bearing exercise increase bone mass. Bone is an active tissue; in response to various signals, the osteoclasts break down old bone and the osteoblasts lay down new bone, a process called *remodeling*.

BONE MATRIX

Bone is made of a matrix of materials, of which one-third is organic (carbon-based) and two-thirds are inorganic. The organic material in bone is primarily a mix of collagen and **glycoproteins**, proteins modified with carbohydrates. Calcium phosphate in a form called **hydroxyapatite** makes up about 85% of the inorganic portion of the matrix, with the remaining 15% composed of a variety of other minerals and ions. Since bone is made of both organic material and inorganic material, it is said to be a **composite material**. The organic portion of bone gives it flexibility, while the inorganic portion provides strength. Both components are essential to function. If bone is depleted of inorganic components, particularly calcium phosphate, it becomes too flexible, almost like rubber. A nutritional disease called **rickets** results from a deficiency of vitamin D, which promotes calcium absorption by the body. When the body is deficient in vitamin D, it cannot regulate calcium and phosphate levels. If the blood level of these minerals becomes too low, calcium and phosphate are released from the bones into the bloodstream in order to elevate the blood levels. Rickets causes a progressive softening and weakening of the bones that eventually can lead to deformities. These are most noticeable in the long bones of the legs, since they bear

HOW BONES GET WEAK: AN EXPERIMENT

Rickets is a disease caused by a lack of vitamin D, which is needed for the body to absorb calcium. When a person has rickets, the bones weaken and become deformed. You can demonstrate the effects of rickets by doing this simple experiment. The next time you have chicken for dinner, set aside the bones from the two drumsticks. Clean the bones as best you can to remove meat and other loose tissue.

Before you proceed, hold each of the drumstick bones (these are the femurs of the chicken) with one thumb and forefinger on each end. Apply a little pressure to make sure that the bones are still solid.

Next, place each of the bones into a separate tall drinking glass or jar. Pour milk into one of the jars until the bone is completely covered. This will be your control. Then, pour vinegar into the container with the other bone until the bone is fully immersed. Vinegar is an acid that will extract, or leach, calcium phosphate from the bone. Cover each container with plastic wrap and label them properly (this is not only good scientific practice, but will also keep someone from drinking your experiment!). Place the containers in the refrigerator for five days.

After the five days, remove both containers from the refrigerator and pour out the liquid. Wash both of the bones with running water until they are clean. First, check the rigidity of the control bone, the one that was soaked in milk. How does it compare to the bones with which you started? Next, test the rigidity of the vinegar-soaked bone. You should notice a substantial difference between the two bones. The one soaked in vinegar should be much softer and weaker, because the vinegar has caused the bone to demineralize. Finally, stand each bone on end and press down from the top the weight of the body. A condition called **brittle bone disease** results when the concentration of the protein component of bone, primarily collagen, is too low. This results in a loose and very weak bone structure that does not contain enough

Figure 6.3 The girl pictured here has rickets, a disease that results from a lack of calcium and/or vitamin D in the diet. Rickets weakens the long bones so that they are not strong enough to support the body; they bend outwardly under the body's weight.

with your thumb. Which bone bends under pressure? What happens to the vinegar-soaked bone is similar to what happens to the leg bones of a person who has rickets!

calcium and breaks easily. In persons with this disease, bones can shatter under weight or stress.

BONE MARROW

The **bone marrow** is the soft tissue found inside the cavities of bones. There are three types of bone marrow: red marrow, yellow marrow, and gelatinous marrow. The ratio of these three types of marrow changes with age and reflects the demands of the body at any given age.

Red bone marrow, or **hemopoietic tissue**, gives rise to blood cells. Just about all of the bone marrow in young children is of this class and reflects the need to produce many blood cells while the body is growing and developing.

Yellow bone marrow contains much more fatty tissue than red bone marrow does. By the time a person reaches middle age, the majority of red bone marrow has become yellow bone marrow. While yellow bone marrow cannot produce blood cells, in an emergency, such as severe anemia, yellow marrow can be converted back to red bone marrow. In adults, most of the red bone marrow that remains is found in the ribs, the vertebrae, the sternum, parts of the pelvic girdle, the heads of the femur where it joins the hip, and the humerus where it joins the shoulder. The primary function for yellow bone marrow may be fat storage.

By the time we reach old age, most of our yellow bone marrow has become **gelatinous bone marrow**. Gelatinous marrow looks like reddish-brown jelly. We do not know of a function for this form of marrow.

OSSIFICATION

In a developing embryo, the "bones" of the skeleton are actually composed of hyaline cartilage and fibrous membrane instead of bone. Ossification is the process by which bone replaces the cartilage (Figure 6.4). Ossification begins with invasion of the cartilage by blood vessels in what will be the diaphysis of the bone, and later, in the epiphyses. Between the two, on each end of the bone, a new region, the metaphysis, is formed. Most bone growth occurs in the metaphysis. Each metaphysis contains five clearly distinct zones, all of which are critical to bone formation:

1. The **zone of reserve cartilage** is the region farthest away from the center of the developing bone. It contains the cartilage that has yet to begin the conversion process.
2. In the **zone of cell proliferation**, the site toward the center of the bone nearest the zone of reserve cartilage, chondrocytes, or cartilage cells, multiply.
3. In the **zone of cell hypertrophy**, the chondrocytes stop dividing. Zones two and three are continually pushing toward the end of the bone, reducing the size of the zone of reserve cartilage.
4. The **zone of calcification** is where the calcification of cartilage occurs. Minerals are deposited between columns of lacunae.
5. The **zone of bone deposition** is where the lacunae begin to break down and the chondrocytes begin to die off. As the lacunae break down, hollow channels are formed that fill with marrow and blood vessels. Osteoclasts dissolve the calcified cartilage, while osteoblasts begin to deposit concentric rings of matrix. As the concentric layers are added, the channels get smaller and smaller. Eventually, the osteoblasts become trapped in the tiny channels and convert to osteocytes, which stops the addition of layers of matrix.

REPAIR OF BONE BREAKS

We have learned that bone is an active tissue. In the case of broken bones, the body has a mechanism for repairing the damaged bone. This process occurs in four stages (Figure 6.5).

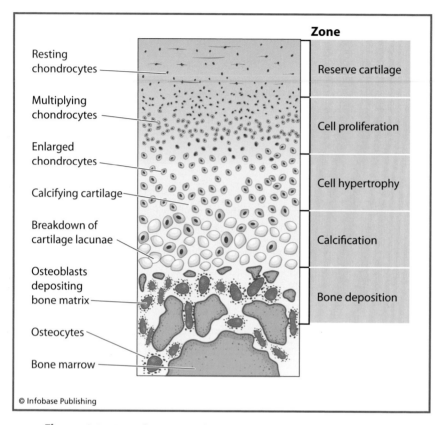

Resting chondrocytes

Multiplying chondrocytes

Enlarged chondrocytes

Calcifying cartilage

Breakdown of cartilage lacunae

Osteoblasts depositing bone matrix

Osteocytes

Bone marrow

Zone

Reserve cartilage

Cell proliferation

Cell hypertrophy

Calcification

Bone deposition

© Infobase Publishing

Figure 6.4   Most bone growth occurs in the metaphysis, which contains five different growth zones–the zones of reserve cartilage, cell proliferation, cell hypertrophy, calcification, and bone deposition.

The first stage is the formation of a **hematoma** at the site of internal bleeding. When a bone fractures, blood vessels in the area are also damaged and blood leaks into the surrounding tissues. The hematoma develops into a blood clot.

The second stage in bone repair is the formation of **granulation tissue**. As blood vessels infiltrate the hematoma, a soft, fibrous tissue is laid down. The site also attracts macrophages (a type of white blood cell), osteoclasts, and osteogenic cells. The osteogenic cells reproduce rapidly within two days of initial injury.

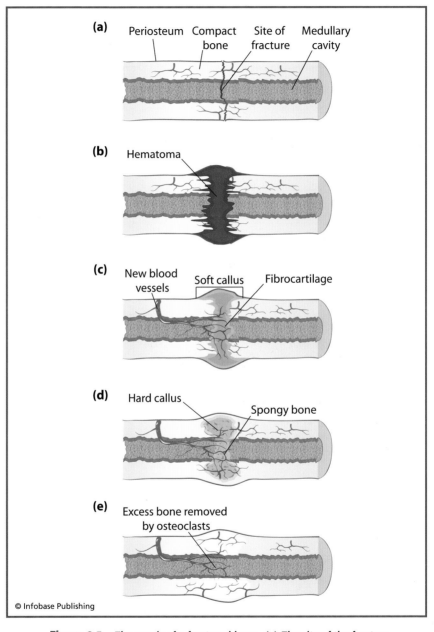

Figure 6.5   The repair of a fractured bone. (a) The site of the fracture. (b) Blood infiltrates the damaged site, forming a hematoma. (c) A soft callus of fibrocartilage forms around the hematoma to provide support. (d) Osteoblasts produce a hard callus to strengthen the soft callus. (e) Osteoclasts remove excess bone and callus.

The third stage in the process is **callus formation**. Several cells are important in this process. Fibroblasts deposit collagen in the granulation tissue. Some of the osteogenic cells differentiate into **chondroblasts**, or collagen-producing cells, which form areas of soft callus tissue made of fibrocartilage. Other osteogenic cells differentiate into osteoblasts, which produce the **hard callus**, a bony collar. The hard callus adheres to the dead bone around the site of injury and acts as a temporary splint to hold the broken ends together. This is why doctors attempt to "set" a broken bone as soon as possible after an injury. Setting the bone positions the broken ends in the most natural position for healing. If the bone is not properly set, the repaired bone may be deformed. It takes about 4 to 6 weeks for the hard callus to form. Because the bone shouldn't move during that time, a broken bone is usually put into a cast or splint to keep the "set" bone in place.

The final step in the process is called **remodeling**. During remodeling, which requires 3 to 4 months, hard callus remains at the site. Osteoclasts dissolve small fragments of bone, and osteoblasts bridge the gap between the broken bone with spongy bone. Eventually, this spongy bone is remodeled to compact bone. Within 4 to 6 months, repair is complete. Generally, the older we are, or the poorer our general health, the greater the length of time for the healing of bone.

CONNECTIONS

In this chapter, we have explored the nature of bone cells and tissues. Using long bones as models, we have explored the structure of bone and have learned about the processes for making new bone and repairing broken bones. We have seen that bones consist of both hard and soft tissues and that both types play a vital role in the function of the skeletal system.

We have also seen that different bones contain different types of marrow and that the distribution of the different types of marrow changes with age. Finally, we have explored the role of various cells in bone growth, both during natural growth and development of the body, and in the repair of broken or otherwise damaged bones.

7

Muscles, Muscle Cells, and Muscle Tissues

THE STUDY OF MUSCLES IS CALLED **myology**. THERE ARE three primary types of muscles: skeletal muscle, smooth muscle, and cardiac muscle. Skeletal muscles are those that are usually attached to bone and are responsible for movement and stability of the body. Skeletal muscles are the focus of Chapter 8. Smooth muscles are associated with various organ systems of the body, including the circulatory, digestive, and urinary systems, where conscious muscle control is neither required nor desirable. Finally, cardiac muscle makes up the walls of the heart. Cardiac muscle has physical characteristics similar to those of skeletal muscle, but cardiac muscle is not under conscious control (Figure 7.1).

GENERAL CHARACTERISTICS OF MUSCLE TISSUES

Even though there are three distinct types of muscles, all muscles have certain characteristics in common. Five traits help to distinguish muscle cells from other cell types in the body.

1. All muscles demonstrate **responsiveness**. Although responsiveness is a property of all living cells, it is particularly notable among muscle cells. As

Figure 7.1 Micrographs of skeletal muscle (*top*), cardiac muscle (*middle*), and smooth muscle (*bottom*). Each type of muscle has a different function.

muscle cells are stimulated by chemical signals, stretching, electrical charge, or other stimuli, the cells respond through an electrical change across their plasma membranes.

2. All muscles exhibit **conductivity**. When one muscle cell is stimulated, the electrical charge it generates across its membrane stimulates the muscle cells on either side of it, which causes the charge to travel along the muscle cells and to communicate the response throughout the muscle tissue.

3. Muscle cells exhibit **contractability**. When stimulated, muscle cells have the ability to shorten, or contract. When this is done in concert with a number of other muscle cells in the same region, the muscles "pull" on bone or other tissues, resulting in movement.

4. Muscle cells exhibit **extendibility**, which is the opposite of contractability, in that the muscles must relax and extend between contractions. Some muscle cells are three times longer when extended than when contracted.

5. All muscle cells must have **elasticity**. When muscles are relaxed, they can be stretched. When the tension causing the muscles to stretch is released, an elastic cell returns to its original length and shape. Very few other cells in the human body have the ability to survive stretching.

SKELETAL MUSCLE

Skeletal muscle tissue has three defining characteristics. First, it is under voluntary control, which means that we can consciously control its movements and functions. Second, skeletal muscle tissue is striated, or striped, when viewed under the microscope. Third, skeletal muscle is usually attached to one or more bones. Typical skeletal muscle cells are about 3.0

centimeters (cm) long and about 100 micrometers (μm) in diameter. Since these cells are so long, they are often referred to as muscle fibers. Smooth muscle is not under voluntary control, is not striated, and is not attached to bone. Finally, cardiac muscle is not under voluntary control and is not attached to bone, but it does have striations.

Skeletal muscles consist of both skeletal muscle tissue and fibrous connective tissue. Each individual muscle fiber is surrounded by the **endomysium**. Bundles of muscle fibers that work together are called **fascicles**. Fascicles, in turn, are surrounded by a connective tissue sheath known as the **perimysium**, and entire muscles are surrounded by a connective tissue sheath known as the **epimysium** (Figure 7.1a). These connective tissues join the collagen fibers of the tendons, and tendons join the collagen of bone matrix, physically linking muscles to bones. As a result, if a muscle contracts, it pulls on the connective tissue, which causes a bone to move.

Collagen, a soft tissue of the body, shares some physical properties with muscle, while differing in other properties. Collagen shares with muscle the characteristics of extensibility and elasticity, but lacks responsiveness, conductivity, and contractability. As a result, collagen can be stretched and restored to its original form, but it cannot do so actively. Muscle must exert force to produce changes in collagen configuration.

Structure of Skeletal Muscle Cells

During embryonic development, muscle cells develop from special stem cells called **myoblasts**. The myoblasts fuse together to form each muscle fiber, and the nuclei fuse to form the long, cylinder-shaped nuclei positioned just below the plasma membrane that are characteristic of skeletal muscle cells. A few of the myoblasts become **satellite cells** that remain associated with muscles and multiply and produce new muscle fibers if muscles become injured and need repair. The plasma membrane of a skeletal muscle cell

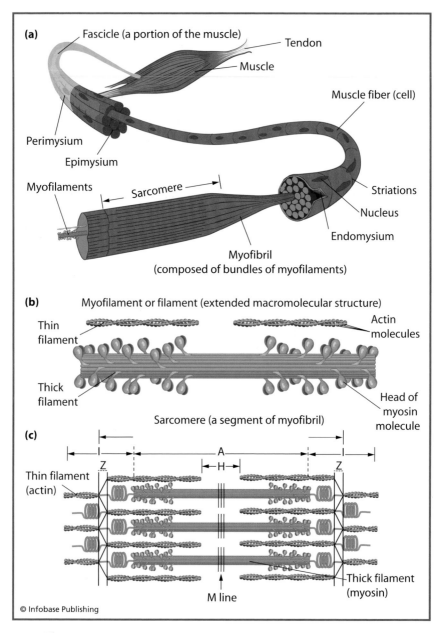

Figure 7.2 Structure of skeletal muscle. Skeletal muscle is made up of muscle fibers, which in turn are made up of myofibrils–fibers that are composed of thick and thin myofilaments. Thick myofilaments are made up of myosin, while thin myofilaments are composed of F actin, G actin, and tropomyosin. The arrangement of the actin and myosin filaments in a sarcomere produces the light and dark bands of skeletal muscle tissue.

is called the **sarcolemma**, while the cytoplasm is known as **sarcoplasm**. The sarcoplasm is filled with protein bundles called **myofibrils** that are about 1 micrometer long. The sarcoplasm also contains large amounts of **glycerol**, a three-carbon alcohol that serves as a source of energy for muscle cells, and a protein called **myoglobin**, which stores oxygen for metabolism. Finally, the smooth endoplasmic reticulum of muscle cells is called the **sarcoplasmic reticulum**. It forms a network around each myofibril with sacs called **terminal cisternae**, which are storage sites for calcium ions. The release of these calcium ions controls muscle contraction.

Myofilaments

The structural units of myofibrils are called **myofilaments** (Figure 7.2b). There are three distinct types of myofilaments. Thick filaments are about 15 nanometers (nm) in diameter and are made up of several hundred myosin molecules. Each myosin molecule is made of two polypeptides and is shaped like a golf club. A typical myofilament contains between 200 and 500 of these units.

Thin filaments are about 7 nm in diameter and are made up of two molecules of a protein called **fibrous actin**, or **F actin**. Each F actin is like a string of beads. The "beads" that make up the F actin are called **globular actin**, or **G actin**. Each G actin can bind to the head of a myosin molecule. The thin filaments each have 40 to 60 molecules of a different protein, **tropomyosin**. When a muscle is relaxed, each tropomyosin molecule blocks several G actin molecules, which prevents binding with the heads of the myosin molecules.

Elastic filaments are about 1 nm in diameter and consist of a protein called titin. Elastic filaments run down the core of thick filaments. The elastic filaments extend from the thick filaments on the ends and serve to anchor the filaments to Z disks. Z disks and elastin fibers are important in keeping the muscle fibers together, which prevents them from overstretching, and play a role in allowing the cells to return to their resting length after being stretched.

Myosin and actin are the contractile proteins of muscles, while tropomyosin and **troponin** (a calcium-binding protein) are the regulatory proteins.

Striations

Skeletal muscle tissue has alternating dark and light bands, or striations that are the result of the arrangement of actin and myosin (Figure 7.2c). These bands form the characteristic striated pattern of skeletal muscles and cardiac muscle. The dark band, which corresponds to the length of the thick filaments, is called the A band, while the light band, where there are only thin filaments, is called the I band. Within the A band is an especially dark region. This is the point where the thick and thin filaments overlap. In the middle of the A band is a lighter region, the H band, which contains thick filaments but not thin ones.

I bands also have a dark line that runs down the center. This dark line is made of Z disks. Recall that the Z disks serve as the anchoring site for the thick filaments and the elastic filaments. The area of the myofibril between adjacent Z disks is called a **sarcomere**, which is the contractile unit for the muscle (Figure 7.3). When a muscle contracts, it does so because the sarcomeres shorten and draw the Z disks closer together. The Z disk is also connected to the sarcolemma. When the Z disks are pulled together, the tension on the sarcolemma makes the entire muscle cell shorten.

MUSCLE CONTRACTION

We have examined the basic structure of muscle cells and have noted that contraction of muscles, at least skeletal muscles, leads to movement, but what causes muscle fibers to contract? In this next section, we will explore some of the more common signals that cause muscles to work.

Nerve Stimulation

Skeletal muscle contracts only upon receiving specific stimuli. The most common stimulus for a muscle is stimulation in

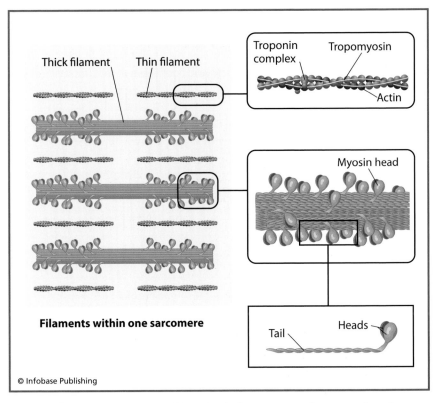

Figure 7.3 The composition of a single sarcomere, the contractile unit for muscle. Muscle contracts and relaxes as the myosin heads move back and forth.

the form of impulses from nerve cells, or neurons. Impulses are regions of electrical and chemical change that travel along the nerve cell membrane. At junctions of a nerve cell with another nerve cell or with a muscle fiber, the impulse is transmitted across a tiny gap by a chemical released by the specialized nerve cell ending. This gap is called a *synapse*.

Muscles are stimulated by impulses from **somatic motor neurons**, which originate in the brain stem and spinal cord. These impulses are carried to the muscles through the axons, the long, thin extensions of these somatic motor neurons. The ends of these axons branch many times. Each branch leads to a different muscle fiber, and each muscle fiber can only be stimulated, or innervated, by one neuron (Figure 7.4). When a motor neuron sends impulses to a muscle, each impulse stimulates about 200 muscle fibers, which are coordinated to contract together. All muscle fibers stimulated to contract from a single neuron form a **motor unit**. This allows one nerve to coordinate contraction of an entire muscle.

What happens if impulses cannot pass from the nerve to the muscle? This might happen for a number of reasons, including damage to the neuron or the presence of a poison that blocks the action of the chemical that transmits impulses across the synapse. In any case, if the impulses do not reach the muscle fibers, the muscle will not contract. Remember that the signal is mostly electrical. You can make a simple model for the nerve/muscle interaction using a battery, a wire, a switch, and a light bulb. When the circuit is complete, electrons flow from the battery through the circuit, including the light bulb, and back to the battery again. If you break the wire along the path, the current cannot flow and the light bulb will not light. If you open the switch (break the contacts so current does not flow), the same thing happens. Damage to the nerve or blocking the communication between the nerve and the muscle has the same effect as breaking the circuit in the electrical model, in that the muscle will not contract if the circuit is broken.

Electrical Stimulation

Muscles can be stimulated to contract by the application of a mild electrical current. Since nerves communicate with muscles electrically, artificially applying an electrical charge across a muscle will also cause it to contract. Doctors sometimes do this to test muscle responsiveness.

Calcium Ion Stimulation

It is possible to short-circuit, or artificially stimulate, a nerve by exposing it to certain chemicals, such as calcium ions (Ca^{++}),

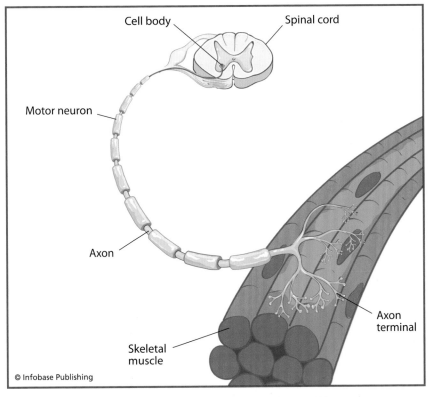

Figure 7.4 A single nerve is able to stimulate multiple muscle fibers. Nerve cells, or neurons, are composed of dendrites that receive information, a cell body, and an axon, which passes on the information. Axons can branch many times and connect to many muscle fibers; thus, one signal can stimulate more than one muscle.

which are stored in neurons. When impulses reach the gate that keeps calcium ions in, the gate opens and the calcium ions flood into the synaptic knob, the structure at the end of a neuron. The increased calcium ions cause the neuron to release a chemical called acetylcholine into the gap between neurons. The acetylcholine stimulates the receptors on the next neuron in the nerve pathway. The stimulation causes impulses to travel along the second neuron to the end, where the synaptic signal is repeated. This is how impulses travel from one neuron to the next or from a neuron to a muscle fiber. Treating muscle tissues with calcium ions stimulates muscle contraction.

THE MECHANICS OF MUSCLE CONTRACTION

We have already noted that contraction of muscles involves shortening of the sarcomere, but how does this happen? Remember that the contraction of a muscle is movement, and movement requires expenditure of energy. The main energy currency for living cells is **ATP (adenosine triphosphate)**.

HOPE FOR HEALING SPINAL CORD INJURIES

Although spinal cord injuries are technically damage to the nervous system, not the muscular system, the constant need for communication between the two systems means that injuries affect them both. Spinal cord injuries are among the most severe. Since the spinal cord is made of nervous tissue, which is not able to regenerate, an injury to the spinal cord is usually permanent. Though we may not be able to reverse spinal injury, modern technology and ongoing medical research offers new hope for overriding the damage to the spinal column.

As our understanding of muscle physiology, electrical engineering, and computer miniaturization develops, there may be hope for those who are paraplegic (paralyzed from the waist down) or quadriplegic (paralyzed from the neck down). New techniques may someday allow us to develop artificial "nerves" using wires and electrodes. With the help of computer chips complex enough to control thousands of functions at once, it may be possible to program a computer to assist people who have spinal cord injuries in stimulating the muscles of the legs, arms, or chest. Such a program would essentially bypass the spinal column and communicate directly with the muscles. More advances have been made in medicine in the past decade than in all of history before that. Robotics, nanotechnology, and human engineering may not only open new doors, but they may actually help some people who are currently in wheelchairs to walk through them!

Figure 7.5 Muscle contraction is driven by the energy released from the breakdown of adenosine triphosphate (ATP) to adenosine diphosphate (ADP) and phosphate.

The last two of its three phosphate groups are bonded to the molecule with high-energy bonds. When those bonds are broken, energy is released. It may not surprise you to learn that contraction of muscles involves the breakdown of ATP.

The "head end" of a myosin molecule has a binding site for ATP (Figure 7.5). In order for myosin to begin the contraction of the sarcomere, ATP must be attached. This binding site has an enzyme near it called myosin ATPase. As the ATPase breaks down ATP, two by-products—ADP (adenosine diphosphate) and phosphate ion—are generated but remain attached to the myosin head. The energy released from ATP is absorbed by the myosin, which moves into an activated, or energized, form. As the ADP and phosphate are released, the myosin goes to the relaxed form, and, as it does, it pulls along the actin chain associated with the myosin head. The head of the myosin remains attached to the actin until a new ATP binds myosin, which causes it to release. As this process is repeated over and over, the myosin crawls along the actin chain toward the middle of the sarcomere. Since myosin heads extend toward the center of the sarcomere from each side, the two ends pull toward the middle, shortening the chain.

A mechanical model for this myosin/actin association is a bicycle chain and its cog. Think of the teeth on the cog as myosin and the chain as actin. When you put energy into the cog, a tooth moves forward, drawing the chain along with it. Add more energy and the chain pulls farther. Now imagine two bicycles connected to the same chain. If you put energy into both by pressing on the pedals, the bicycles will be drawn toward each other, shortening the distance between them.

CARDIAC MUSCLE

Cardiac muscle is found only in the heart. Like skeletal muscle, it is striated, but for a different reason. Cardiac muscle striations are due to *intercalated discs*, which form the thick, dark lines in the muscles. Intercalated discs are a specialized type of junction between cells. They are described as electrical gap junctions, and they allow each cell to stimulate its neighboring cells electrically. The heart contains a specialized structure called a **pacemaker**, which initiates electrical impulses at a fixed rhythm. This means that cardiac muscle can be stimulated to contract without a signal from a nerve. The electrical charge travels over the heart in a wave, causing the various chambers to contract in a coordinated fashion. This squeezes blood through the heart and drives blood circulation.

Another important difference between cardiac muscle and skeletal muscle is the number and size of the mitochondria, the organelles that are the site of ATP production. The large mitochondria of cardiac muscle make up about 25% of the volume of the muscle, whereas the smaller mitochondria of skeletal muscles make up only about 2% of the volume. The cardiac muscle mitochondria use a wider range of energy sources than skeletal muscle mitochondria, but are much more sensitive to the depletion of oxygen. Most heart attacks occur when the oxygen supply to the cardiac muscle is interrupted. The energy level in the cardiac tissue drops and the heart ceases to function normally.

SMOOTH MUSCLE

Smooth muscle can be divided into two types: multiunit smooth muscle and single-unit smooth muscle. Multiunit smooth muscle is located in the walls of the large arteries, in the pulmonary air passages, in the iris of the eye, and in the piloerector muscles of hair follicles. A separate terminal branch from the nerve (in this case, a nerve from the involuntary nervous system) is attached to each cell, as in the skeletal muscles discussed earlier, so that impulses travel to a cluster of muscle cells, which make up a motor unit.

A more common mechanism for control of smooth muscle is the single-unit smooth muscle, which is found in the digestive, urinary, respiratory, and reproductive tracts, as well as in most blood vessels. With single-unit smooth muscle, two nerve patterns exist. The inner track innervates muscle cells that form a ring around the organ, while the outer track is longitudinal, with muscle cells running lengthwise along the organ. These muscle cells are considered single-unit because they do not each have a nerve branch. Instead, they have gap junctions (like cardiac cells) that allow the cells to stimulate each other. This means that a large number of cells contract together, almost as if they constituted a single muscle cell.

Although smooth muscle, like cardiac muscle, is controlled by the involuntary nervous system, and we therefore have no control over the process, there are stimuli that affect the contraction of smooth muscle. For instance, some of the smooth muscles of the respiratory system and circulatory system are stimulated by concentrations of oxygen and carbon dioxide. Acid levels affect contraction of smooth muscle in the digestive system. Still other smooth muscle may be stimulated by hormones or stretch responses (in the stomach and bladder).

CONNECTIONS

Three basic types of muscles exist in the human body. Skeletal muscle is generally under our conscious control, has a striated appearance, is generally attached to bones, and is involved in movement. Cardiac muscle, which is found only in the heart, is also striated, but is not under conscious control. Smooth muscle lacks striations, is not under voluntary control, and is found in the walls of blood vessels and many organs of the digestive and urinary systems. All muscles contain myosin and actin and use ATP as the source of energy for movement, and all muscles share the same basic mechanism of contraction.

8

Skeletal Muscles

As we saw in Chapter 1, skeletal muscles work in opposing pairs to move the skeleton and, therefore, the body. Thus, the first function of the muscles is to carry out **voluntary movement**, movement that is under conscious control. Skeletal muscles also function in stabilization of the body. Although the skeleton provides rigid support for the body, the muscles, by balancing the pull of opposing pairs, act to stabilize the bones and therefore hold the body in place. Our posture is dependent on the stabilizing effect of the muscles. Attachment of muscles to vital organs helps to hold those organs in place. A visual analogy is the Golden Gate Bridge in San Francisco, California, a classic example of a suspension bridge. Massive cables connect the main platform of the bridge to the metal structure that suspends it. These cables stabilize the platform to the frame, much as the muscles stabilize the bones of the skeleton and the vital organs to the bones or other tissues.

Among the voluntary movements involving skeletal muscles are those involved in communication. The muscles of the face, especially those of the jaw and tongue, are incredibly complex. The intricate control and movement of these muscles, along with

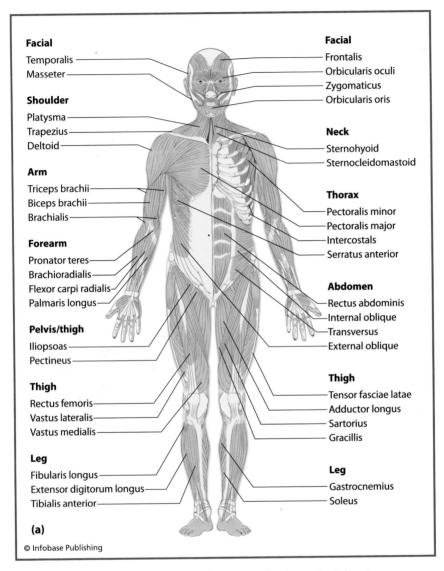

Figure 8.1 The human muscular system is shown in (*above*) an anterior view and (*next page*) a posterior view. The muscles, along with the bones, provide support and allow the body to move. The body has

(*continues on page 99*)

those of the larynx, or voice box, allow us to make the multitude of sounds that lead to verbal communication. People who are mute (unable to speak) can also communicate through sign language

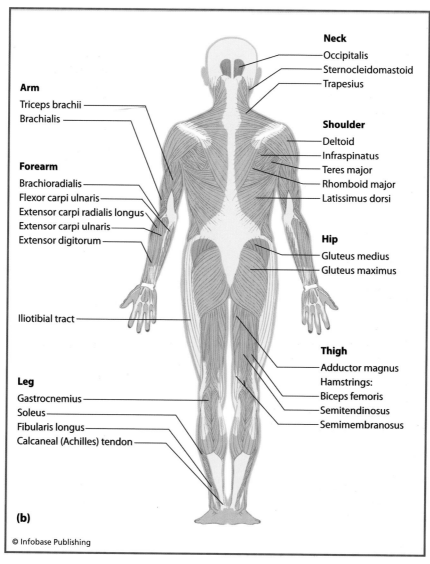

Neck
Occipitalis
Sternocleidomastoid
Trapesius

Arm
Triceps brachii
Brachialis

Shoulder
Deltoid
Infraspinatus
Teres major
Rhomboid major
Latissimus dorsi

Forearm
Brachioradialis
Flexor carpi ulnaris
Extensor carpi radialis longus
Extensor carpi ulnaris
Extensor digitorum

Hip
Gluteus medius
Gluteus maximus

Iliotibial tract

Thigh
Adductor magnus
Hamstrings:
Biceps femoris
Semitendinosus
Semimembranosus

Leg
Gastrocnemius
Soleus
Fibularis longus
Calcaneal (Achilles) tendon

(b)

several different types of muscle, from the powerful muscles that move the arms and legs to the smaller, more delicate muscles that open and close the eyelids.

by using the muscles of the hands and arms to create equally intricate and subtle movements. Without our muscular system, human communication as we know it would not be possible.

Skeletal muscles also function in the generation of heat. Muscle cells burn large amounts of **glucose**, a simple sugar that is the primary fuel for the cells of our bodies. The energy from the chemical breakdown of glucose is used to produce ATP, which in turn provides the energy for muscle movement. Heat is generated as a by-product. This is why you become overheated from intense or prolonged exercise. Your skeletal muscles are generating more heat than the body needs to maintain its normal temperature. Under conditions of extreme cold, the voluntary muscles undergo an involuntary process called **shivering**, where the muscles undergo uncontrolled spasms. The body triggers shivering if the temperature of the trunk of the body begins to drop. Shivering generates heat and helps to maintain normal body temperature.

GENERAL MUSCLE ANATOMY

Muscles come in a variety of shapes and perform a variety of functions. As a general rule, most skeletal muscles attach to bones or other structures at two sites. One attachment site is relatively immobile, while the other attachment site is much more mobile. The relatively immobile, or stationary, end of a muscle is called the **origin**, while the more mobile end of the same muscle is known as the **insertion**. Many muscles tend to be wider in the middle and taper toward the origin and the insertion. This thickened middle area is called the **belly**.

Figure 8.1 shows the general structure of the human muscular system. The more than 600 muscles of the human body can be divided into 5 groups based on the arrangement of the bundles of muscle fibers. The groups are fusiform, parallel, convergent, pennate, and circular muscles (Figure 8.2).

Fusiform Muscles

Fusiform muscles are spindle-shaped—tapered on the ends and thicker in the middle. Since this design concentrates the

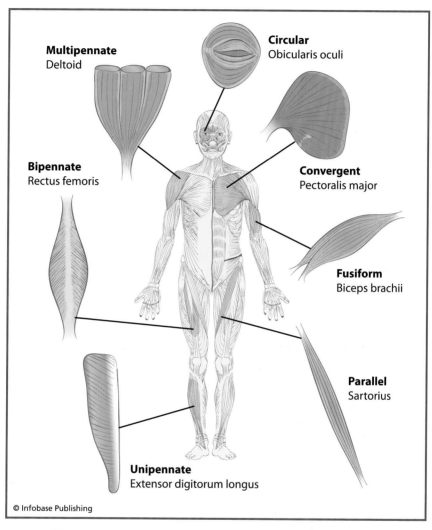

Multipennate
Deltoid

Circular
Obicularis oculi

Bipennate
Rectus femoris

Convergent
Pectoralis major

Fusiform
Biceps brachii

Parallel
Sartorius

Unipennate
Extensor digitorum longus

© Infobase Publishing

Figure 8.2   There are five different types of muscles: fusiform, parallel, convergent, pennate, and circular. Their unique shapes and the ways they connect to the bones allow a wide range of movement.

strength of a large bundle of muscles at relatively small origins and insertions, fusiform muscles tend to be strong. The biceps muscle of the upper arm is a fusiform muscle.

Parallel Muscles

As the name suggests, **parallel muscles** have bundles of fascicles that are essentially equally wide at the origin, the insertion, and the belly. These muscles form belt-like structures. In the relaxed state, parallel muscles can be quite long. Although they can shorten more than fusiform muscles, relative to their relaxed length, they tend to be less strong than fusiform muscles. The muscles of the abdomen are parallel muscles.

Convergent Muscles

Convergent muscles are shaped like a fan. They are wide at the origin and narrow at the insertion. The strength of a large number of fascicles concentrated at the insertion makes convergent muscles quite strong. The pectoralis major muscle of the chest is a convergent muscle.

Pennate Muscles

Pennate muscles are shaped like feathers. The bundles of muscle fibers insert onto a tendon that runs the length of the muscle. Pinnate muscles can be further divided into three groups. **Unipennate muscles** are those in which the fascicles all attach from the same side. The palmar interosseous muscle in the palm is a unipennate muscle. **Bipennate muscles** have bundles of muscle fibers that attach to the tendon from two sides with the tendon in the middle. The rectus femoris muscle of the thigh is a bipennate muscle. **Multipennate muscles** are shaped like several feathers that have all their quills joining at a single point. An example of a multipennate muscle is the deltoid muscle of the shoulder.

Circular (Sphincter) Muscles

Circular, or **sphincter, muscles** form rings around various openings in the body. The muscles around the lips and the eyelids are circular muscles.

WORKING IN GROUPS

Body movements usually do not involve the action of a single muscle alone. More often, groups of muscles coordinate their actions to provide a smooth, even movement. As a general rule, the muscles that work together as a functional group fall into four major categories.

Agonist Muscles

The muscle that exerts the majority of force in a movement is known as the **agonist**, or **primary mover**. When you bend your elbow, the biceps muscle is the agonist.

Synergist Muscles

Most agonist muscles have other muscles that aid their motion. Muscles that work additively to the agonist are known as **synergist** muscles. In addition to adding strength to the agonist, the synergist helps to stabilize the movement or to restrict the range of movement of the agonist.

Antagonist Muscles

Since muscles can only pull, not push, to reverse the action of the agonist, a complementary muscle or group of muscles must work in the opposite direction. An **antagonist** muscle works in opposition to the agonist. In addition to returning the body part to the original position, antagonists fine-tune the control of the agonist. They moderate the speed and the range of the agonist, which helps to protect the body from damage to muscles or joints. The triceps muscle along the back of the upper arm is the antagonist to the biceps. It is important to remember that while the biceps is the agonist and the triceps is the antagonist when the elbow is bent, their roles reverse when the elbow is straightened—that is, the triceps becomes the agonist and the biceps the antagonist.

Fixator Muscles

Fixator muscles are those that prevent a bone from moving in an unwanted direction. For instance, when you want to bend your elbow, the biceps muscle does the most of the work. The biceps connects to the shoulder blade, or scapula, at its origin and on the radius at its insertion. Fixator muscles attached to the scapula prevent it from moving when the biceps contracts to ensure that the energy of the biceps is concentrated on moving the radius, not the shoulder blade.

MUSCLES OF THE FACE

Generally, the muscles of the face are small and short to allow tremendous precision and control, but not a significant amount of strength. The exceptions to this rule are the muscles of the jaw, which are extremely strong. Facial muscles control facial expression, chewing, swallowing, and, in part, speech.

Muscles of Facial Expression

The muscles that control facial expression are much more highly developed in primates than they are in other animals. The mouth is the most sensitive structure of facial expression. It is surrounded by a circular muscle responsible for closing the lips. A similar circular muscle surrounds each eye and allows the eyelids to close. The other muscles of the mouth radiate outward from the mouth like spokes on a wheel. The origins of the muscles tend to be away from the mouth, while the insertions are attached to the skin rather than to bone. This combination of specialized structures and anchoring to soft tissue allows for countless and subtle facial expressions, from smiles to frowns to pouts.

Chewing and Swallowing

The tongue is one of the strongest and most flexible structures in the human body. It has sets of muscles originating and terminating within the tongue (intrinsic muscles), and muscles that connect the tongue to other parts of the neck and head (external muscles). The tongue plays a vital role in digestion, as it, along with the muscles of the cheeks, moves food around the mouth. The tongue also delivers the chewed food to the back of the throat, where it enters the esophagus.

The action of chewing is controlled by four paired **muscles of mastication**, or the act of biting and grinding food in your mouth. Two of these that attach at or near the mandible are among the strongest muscles of the body. They allow us to bite and to chew our food. The other two pairs of chewing muscles are important in moving the mandible from side to side for the grinding of food by the molars. Also important for chewing and swallowing are eight pairs of **hyoid muscles**, which are muscles associated with the **hyoid bone**, a U-shaped bone at the base of the tongue that supports the muscles.

As food enters the *pharynx*, the back of the throat, three pairs of muscles known as the *pharyngeal constrictors* contract and force the food down the esophagus.

The larynx also has intrinsic muscles that control the vocal cords, and thus are essential for speech. These muscles also control the opening of the larynx itself to prevent food or fluids from entering the trachea.

Muscles That Control the Head

The bones of the skull are very heavy. Consequently, the muscles that control and support the head must be very strong. There are two major groups of muscles for the head: flexors and extensors. All muscles in these groups have their inserts on cranial bones and their origins on the vertebrae, the thoracic cage, or the pectoral girdle. The flexors draw the head downward toward the body. These muscles are generally located along the sides of the neck. The extensors extend the neck and rotate the head. The extensor muscles are located at the back of the neck. In general, **flexors** act to decrease the angle at a joint, while **extensors** increase the angle at a joint. For example, the biceps muscle is a flexor of the lower arm, while the triceps, the muscle on the back of the upper arm, is an extensor.

MUSCLES OF THE TRUNK

The muscles of the trunk include the muscles of the abdomen, the muscles of the back, and the muscles of respiration (see Figure 8.1).

Muscles of the Abdomen

The abdominal muscles consist of four pairs of muscles that form strong sheets. These muscles serve a number of functions. First, they work with the back muscles to hold the body upright and support the weight of the chest cage, arms, and head. Second, they support and protect the spinal column. Third, they hold and support the internal organs. Fourth, they assist with the vital functions of breathing, waste removal, and reproduction.

The role of protecting organs is vital because, unlike the lungs and heart, which are surrounded by a bony cage, the organs of the abdomen are not protected by hard bone. Thus, the abdominal muscles must be strong in order to insulate

SEE WHAT YOU HAVE LEARNED

In this chapter, we looked at selected muscle groups and how they function. Because of space and time, we did not look at the muscles of the arms and legs. Choose one of these sets of muscles and then find a good anatomy and physiology text (see the Bibliography for suggestions). Pick one of the arm or leg muscle groups and try to identify the agonists, antagonists, synergists, and fixators for each group. Ask yourself these basic questions to guide you:

• What is the primary function of the muscle group?

• How is this process reversed?

• Does the agonist need stabilizing and, if so, what muscles are likely to do this?

• Do the bones need stabilizing and, if so, by what?

    You may be surprised at how much you already know.

and protect the organs—the stomach, liver, spleen, and intestines—that are located in the abdominal cavity.

Muscles of the Back

The muscles of your back also serve a number of functions. They work as antagonists to the abdominal muscles to help control the movement of bending forward. They enable the body to return to an erect posture after bending at the waist. They also work together with the abdominal muscles to maintain an upright posture. Back muscles fall into two groups. Superficial muscles of the back connect the ribs to the vertebrae, while the deep muscles of the back connect the vertebrae to one another.

The primary mover of the back and spine is the erector spinae. This is the bundle of muscles and tendons that causes you to straighten after you bend at the waist. This muscle group can be divided into three sections: the iliocostalis group, which assists with breathing by driving inhalation; the spinalis group; and the longissimus group. All three groups assist with extension or flexing of the vertebrae. The muscles of the longissimus group are concentrated in the lower back, while the other two groups are concentrated in the mid to upper back.

Muscles of Respiration

Three basic muscle groups drive the respiration process. The **diaphragm** is a sheet of muscle that defines the bottom of the chest cavity and separates it from the abdominal cavity. In addition to the diaphragm, there are 11 pairs of external intercostal muscles, located between the ribs and just below the skin, and 11 pairs of internal intercostal muscles, also located between the ribs, but below the layer of the external intercostals. You may be surprised to learn that the lungs themselves do not contain skeletal muscles. The role of the lungs in the inhalation and exhalation process is purely passive.

In inspiration (breathing in), the diaphragm contracts, causing it to flatten and to lower slightly, and the external intercostals contract, lifting the ribs up and away from the lungs. Altogether, the actions of the external intercostals and the diaphragm enlarge the chest cavity, creating a vacuum and pulling on the tissue of the lungs. The lungs, which are flexible in a healthy human, stretch, opening the air sacs within, and air rushes in from the mouth and nose to fill the space.

When the muscles of the diaphragm and external intercostals relax, the weight of the chest cage causes the chest cavity to collapse inward, passively forcing out the air in the lungs. The role of the internal intercostal muscles is in forcible exhalation. For example, if you want to blow up a balloon, simply relaxing the diaphragm and the external intercostals will not provide enough force. The needed force comes from the internal intercostals, which contract, pulling the ribs toward each other and toward the lungs. This forces air out of the lungs and creates the air pressure you need to inflate that balloon or to blow out candles at a birthday party.

CONNECTIONS

In this chapter, we have explored the general anatomy of muscles. We have seen how muscles work in groups to create smooth, fluid motions and how some muscles are designed for strength, while others are designed for delicate, accurate movements. We have learned that while many muscles connect to bone, others can connect to softer tissues to allow for subtle movements. We have learned that muscles usually work in opposing pairs and that these pairs not only can reverse the action of the opposite muscle group, but can also control the intensity of a movement. We have learned that some muscles are used to stabilize the movements of bone and other muscles, thus creating smooth, graceful movements.

Whether they are used for power, as one observes in a weightlifter, or grace, as one observes in a ballet dancer, the skeletal muscles allow us to move our body in an almost endless range of motions.

Appendix: Conversion Chart

Unit (metric)		Metric to English	English to Metric
LENGTH			
Kilometer	km	1 km 0.62 mile (mi)	1 mile (mi) 1.609 km
Meter	m	1 m 3.28 feet (ft)	1 foot (ft) 0.305 m
Centimeter	cm	1 cm 0.394 inches (in)	1 inch (in) 2.54 cm
Millimeter	mm	1 mm 0.039 inches (in)	1 inch (in) 25.4 mm
Micrometer	μm	1 - millionth meter	
WEIGHT (MASS)			
Kilogram	kg	1 kg 2.2 pounds (lbs)	1 pound (lb) 0.454 kg
Gram	g	1 g 0.035 ounces (oz)	1 ounce (oz) 28.35 g
Milligram	mg	1 mg 0.000035 ounces (oz)	
Microgram	μg	1 - millionth gram	
VOLUME			
Liter	L	1 L 1.06 quarts	1 gallon (gal) 3.785 L
			1 quart (qt) 0.94 L
			1 pint (pt) 0.47 L
Milliliter	mL or cc	1 mL 0.034 fluid ounce (fl oz)	1 fluid ounce 29.57 mL (fl oz)
Microliter	μL	1 - millionth liter	
TEMPERATURE			
		$F = 9/5°C + 32$	$°C = 5/9 (°F - 32)$

Glossary

Acromion   The outermost and upward point of the shoulder-blade where the collarbone attaches to the scapula.

Adenosine triphosphate (ATP)   The high-energy molecule that serves as energy currency for cell metabolism.

Agonist   The muscle in a working group that exerts most of the force.

Amino acids   The nitrogen-containing basic building blocks of proteins.

Amphiarthrosis   A joint with limited freedom of movement; plural, *amphiarthroses.*

Anemia   A condition in which the blood contains too few red blood cells that results from the underproduction of red blood cells by the bone marrow stem cells.

Ankle bones   A cluster of short bones at the junction of the lower leg and foot.

Antagonist   The muscle in a working group that works in opposition to the agonist.

Antebrachium   The forearm, extending from the elbow to the wrist.

Appendicular skeleton   The bones of the shoulders, arms, and hands, and the hips, legs, and feet, which are all attached to the axial skeleton.

Arthrology   The study of joints.

Articular cartilage   Hyaline cartilage found where bones meet.

Articular facets   Indentations in the radius that articulate with the bones of the wrist.

Articulate   To form a joint.

ATP   *See* Adenosine triphosphate.

Axial skeleton   The bones of the skull, thoracic cage, and spinal column.

Ball-and-socket joint   A synovial joint consisting of a rounded end on one bone that fits into a cup on the other; this joint allows a wide range of motion.

Base   The end of the metacarpal closest to the wrist.

Belly   The thickened middle area of many muscles.

Biaxial joint   A joint that allows movement in two directions.

Bipennate muscle   A muscle in which muscle fibers connect on both sides of a central ligament.

Body   The shaft of a metacarpal.

Bone marrow   Soft tissue found within bones where blood cells are produced.

Bone marrow stem cell   A cell in bone marrow that gives rise to blood cells.

Bony joint   A fused joint between two previously independent bones.

Bony thorax   The cage of bone that surrounds the chest cavity; consists of the thoracic vertebrae, ribs, and sternum (breastbone).

Brachium   The upper arm, extending from the shoulder to the elbow.

Brittle bone disease   A disease that results in breaking of bones due to too little organic material.

Bursa   Fluid-filled pads found between muscles or where tendons pass over bone; plural, *bursae.*

Calcaneus   The largest tarsal bone; also known as the heel bone.

Callus formation   The development of hard tissue that creates a temporary splint at a bone break.

Canals   Narrow tubes or channels in and between bones.

Capitate   The most rectangular bone of the wrist.

Capitulum   The condyle that contacts the radius.

Cardiac muscle   Striated muscle found in the heart walls; not under conscious control.

Carpal bones   The bones of the wrist.

Carpus   The wrist, consisting of eight small bones.

Cartilage   Skeletal tissue that is softer than bone; does not contain high concentrations of calcium phosphate.

Cartilaginous joint   A joint at which the bones are joined together by cartilage.

Cavity   A hole or canal within the skull.

Centrum   The porous core of a vertebra.

Cervical curvature   The natural curvature of the cervical vertebrae toward the front of the body.

Cervical vertebrae   The top seven vertebrae in the spinal column.

Chitin   A structural compound commonly found in the exoskeleton of insects and crustaceans.

Chondroblast   A cell that produces collagen.

Circular muscle   *See* Sphincter muscle.

Clavicle   A thin, long bone that extends along the front of the shoulder; part of the pectoral girdle; the collarbone.

Coccyx   Four fused vertebrae at the bottom of the spinal column that make up the "tailbone."

Collagen   Fibrous protein that is the main connective tissue for bones and muscles.

Collagen fiber   Tough connective tissue that contributes strength and resilience to bone.

Collarbone   *See* Clavicle.

Compact bone   Bone containing lots of calcium phosphate; dense bone.

Composite material   A material made of two or more distinct components.

Conductivity   The ability of muscle cells and nerve cells to communicate with neighboring cells.

Condyles   Two small bumps on the distal (elbow) end of the humerus and the femur.

Condyloid joints   A biaxial joint in the base of the fingers that allows the finger to move up and down and side to side.

Connective tissue   Tissue consisting of ground substance, fibers, and living cells.

Contractability   The ability of muscle cells to shorten, or contract.

Convergent muscle   Fan-shaped muscle that is wide at the orgin and narrow at the point of insertion.

Coracoid process   A fingerlike piece of bone on the scapula that serves as the attachment point for the biceps and other arm muscles.

Costal cartilage   The pieces of cartilage that join the ribs to the sternum.

Cranial base   The bottom part of the cranium on which the brain rests.

Cranial cavity   The chamber created by the cranial vault and cranial base.

Cranial vault   A chamber surrounded by bone that encloses and protects the brain.

Cranium   The flat bones of the skull that surround and protect the brain.

Crural region   The lower leg, between the knee and ankle.

Cuboid   The largest bone in the distal row of the ankle.

Cuneiforms   Three of the four bones of the distal row of the ankle (the fourth is the cuboid).

Diaphragm   A sheet of muscle that separates the chest cavity from the abdominal cavity and assists in the breathing process.

Diaphysis   The shaft of a long bone.

Diarthrosis   A joint with a high degree of freedom of movement; plural, *diarthroses*.

Differentiation   Conversion of one cell type to another, as in the case of osteogenic cells giving rise to osteoblasts.

Digits   The fingers and toes.

Diploë   The middle, spongy layer of flat bones of the skull.

Elasticity   The ability of muscle cells to stretch and return to the original shape and size.

Endomysium   A fibrous connective tissue surrounding each individual muscle fiber.

Endoskeleton   A rigid, tough support structure on the inside of an organism.

Endosteum   The membrane found inside the canals within bone.

Ends   The two ends of a long bone with the shaft of the bone between them.

Epicondyles   Two bony complexes that flare out on the humerus just above the condyles.

Epimysium   A connective tissue sheath that surrounds entire muscles.

Epiphysis   The end of a long bone; plural, *epiphyses*.

Erythrocyte   A red blood cell.

Exoskeleton   The rigid, tough, outer protective covering of some invertebrate animals.

Extendibility   The ability of muscle cells to elongate.

Extensors   The muscles of the back of the neck that move the head up and backward.

F actin   *See* Fibrous actin.

False ribs   A rib that connects to the sternum indirectly through additional pieces of cartilage.

Fascicle   A bundle of muscle fibers that work together.

Femoral region   The thigh region of the leg.

Femur   The bone of the thigh.

Fibrocartilage   A type of connective tissue that is composed mainly of collagen fibers and is more fibrous than regular cartilage.

Fibrous actin   Polymers of globular actin essential for muscle contraction.

Fibrous joint   A joint where the collagen fiber from one bone extends and integrates into the adjacent bone.

Fibula   The thinner bone of the lower leg that acts as a lateral strut.

Fissure   A crevasse or gorge between bones.

Fixator   The muscle in a working group that prevents a bone from moving in an unwanted direction.

Flat bone   A bone that has a platelike shape, narrow in one dimension and wide in the other two.

Flexors   The muscles on the side of the neck that bend the head down and forward.

Floating ribs   The two lower ribs, 11 and 12, that do not connect to the sternum.

Foramen magnum   The hole in the base of the skull through which the spinal cord passes.

Foramina   Cavities that are classified as holes.

Forensic science   The science of studying evidence from a crime scene in an effort to determine facts about the crime or the victim.

Fossa Ridge   The ridge where bones come together, as in the cranial fossa; plural, *fossae.*

Fusiform muscle   A spindle-shaped muscle that is thicker in the middle than at the ends.

G actin   *See* Globular actin.

Gelatinous bone marrow   Bone marrow of unknown function that accumulates with age.

Glenoid cavity   The cuplike indentation where the ball of the humerus joins the scapula in the shoulder joint.

Gliding joint   A type of synovial joint in which the ends of the bones slide over each other.

Globular actin   Individual spherical-shaped molecules of actin.

Glucose   A simple sugar that is the primary source of energy for the cells of the body.

Glycerol   A three-carbon alcohol that serves as a source of energy for muscle cells.

Glycoprotein   A protein modified with carbohydrates.

Gomphoses   The joints that hold teeth in their sockets.

Granulation tissue   A soft, fibrous tissue laid down during bone repair.

Ground substance   One of three components of connective tissue.

Hallux   The large toe.

Hamate   The wristbone at the base of the little finger.

Hamulus   A hook of bone on the finger end of the hamate.

Hard callus   A bony collar that forms during bone repair.

Haversian canal   The opening in the middle of an osteon.

Head   The end of the metacarpal closest to the finger or thumb.

Hematoma   The site of internal bleeding.

Hematopoiesis   The process by which bone marrow stem cells give rise to new blood cells.

Hemopoietic tissue   The tissue that gives rise to blood cells; also known as red bone marrow.

Hinge joints   Synovial joints that move in one direction, usually with a 90–180° range of motion.

Hip bones   A series of flat bones that are fused to form the pelvic girdle.

Humerus   The long bone of the upper arm, or brachium.

Hyaline cartilage   The type of cartilage found at cartilaginous joints called synchondroses.

Hydroxyapatite   The form of calcium phosphate found in bone.

Hyoid bone   A U-shaped bone or series of bones located between the base of the tongue and the larynx.

Hyoid muscles   Muscles involved with chewing and swallowing that are associated with the hyoid bone.

Ilium   The bone of the os coxae that is largest and closest to the head.

Insertion   The more mobile end of a muscle.

Interosseous membrane   A ligament that connects the radius to the ulna or the tibia to the fibula.

Involuntary muscle   A muscle that is not under conscious control.

Irregular bone   A bone that does not fit into any of the other three categories.

Ischium   The bone of the os coxae that is toward the back of the body and toward the feet.

Joint   A point where two bones come together; bending of body parts usually happens at joints.

Joint capsule   A fibrous capsule filled with synovial fluid that surrounds a synovial joint.

Jugular notch   An indentation in the bone at the top of the sternum.

Kneecap   A sesamoid bone positioned over the knee joint.

Knuckle   The rounded head of the metacarpal seen when a fist is made.

Lacuna   A small space in bone that contains an osteocyte; plural, *lacunae.*

Lap suture   A suture in which the bones have beveled edges that overlap.

Larynx   The cartilaginous structure in the throat that houses the vocal cords; the voice box.

Leukemia   A cancer of the blood that results from the overproduction of white blood cells by the bone marrow stem cells.

Leukocyte   A white blood cell.

Ligament   A piece of connective tissue that joins two bones and allows them to move relative to each other.

Line of symmetry   An imaginary line that can be drawn through the body and that defines the center for a pair of mirror images across the body.

Long bone   A bone that is noticeably longer in one dimension than in the other two.

Lumbar vertebrae   The section of vertebrae, usually 5 in number, between the thoracic vertebrae and the sacrum.

Lunate   A moon-shaped bone of the wrist.

Mandible   The jawbone; it serves as the anchor site for the lower teeth.

Manus   The hand.

Mastication   Chewing; the act of biting and grinding food in the mouth.

Maxilla   The bone extending down from the nasal bone that serves as the anchor site for the upper teeth.

Medial epicondyle   The epicondyle that houses the ulnar nerve and is commonly called the "funny bone."

Medial line   The line of symmetry that runs from the center of the skull through the groin and that divides the body into left and right halves.

Medullary cavity   A hollow cylinder in bone that contains marrow.

Meniscus   A fluid-filled pad found between bones.

Metacarpals   The five bones of the palm.

Mineralization   The incorporation of calcium phosphate into connective tissue, resulting in the formation of bone.

Molt   The periodic shedding of the exoskeleton to allow growth.

Monaxial joint   A joint that moves only in one direction.

Motor unit   All muscles fibers innervated or stimulated by a single neuron.

Multiaxial joint   A joint that moves in many directions.

Multipennate muscle   A muscle that is shaped like a group of several feathers joined by their quills at a single point.

Muscles of facial expression   The muscles of the face that control facial expression.

Muscles of mastication   The muscles used in chewing.

Myoblasts   Individual muscle stem cells that join together into muscle fibers.

Myofibrils   Protein bundles within sarcoplasm.

Myofilaments   The structural units of myofibrils.

Myoglobin   A protein in muscle cells that stores oxygen for energy production.

Myology   The study of muscles.

Nasal bone   A ridge of bone at the top of the nose where the nose joins to the skull.

Navicular   The triangular bone of the ankle.

Opposing pairs   Muscles or muscle groups that operate at the same joint, reversing the movements at the joint and modulating the intensity of movements.

Orbits   The two cavities within the skull that house the eyes.

Origin   The relatively immobile or stationary end of a muscle.

Os coxae   The hipbone formed by the fusion of three bones— the ilium, the ischium, and the pubis; plural, *ossa coxae*.

Osseous tissue   Bone.

Ossification   The formation of hard bone.

Osteoblast   A bone-building cell.

Osteoclast   A bone-destroying cell.

Osteocyte   An osteoblast that has become trapped in the bone matrix; communicates between osteoblasts and osteoclasts.

Osteogenic cell   A rapidly reproducing bone stem cell that gives rise to osteoblasts.

Osteogenic layer   The innermost layer of the periosteum that contains the cells for bone growth.

Osteon   The cylindrical outer portion of channels in bone, made of concentric rings; it runs parallel to the longest dimension of the bone.

Pacemaker   A special tissue in the heart that generates an electrical charge, causing the heart to beat.

Parallel muscle   A muscle with bundles of fascicles that are essentially equally wide at the origin, insertion, and belly.

Paraplegia   A condition in which the lower limbs are paralyzed, usually from the waist down; most often resulting from a spinal cord injury.

Patella   The kneecap, a sesamoid bone.

Pectoral girdle   The spinal column and upper portion of the thoracic cage that serve for the attachment of the shoulders and arms.

Pedal region   The foot.

Pedicle   A projection of bone to which other bones, muscles, or tendons can articulate.

Pelvis (Pelvic girdle)   The fused flat bones in the hip region that support the abdominal organs.

Pennate muscles   Muscles that form an angle in relation to the tendon and pull at an angle, which means that the muscles cannot move their tendons as far as parallel muscles do.

Perimysium   A connective tissue sheath surrounding fascicles.

Periodontal ligament   A strong band of connective tissue that holds the tooth firmly to the jaw.

Periosteum   The double-layered membrane that surrounds bones except at the joint surface.

Phalanges   The bones of the fingers, thumb, and toes; singular, *phalanx*.

Phalanx   The singular form of *phalanges* (the bones of the fingers, thumb, and toes).

Pisiform   A pea-shaped bone of the wrist.

Pivot joint   A monaxial joint where a projection from one bone fits into a ring of ligament on the other.

Plane sutures   Sutures occurring where two bones form straight, nonoverlapping connections.

Primary mover   The muscle in a working group that exerts the majority of force.

Processes   Projections of bone extending from vertebrae that are points of contact with other vertebrae and points of attachment for muscles.

Proteoglycans   Polymers of sugar modified with amino acids.

Pubis   The bone of the os coxae that is toward the front of the body and toward the feet.

Quadriplegia   A condition in which all four limbs are paralyzed, usually resulting from damage to the spinal cord in the cervical region.

Radius   The smaller of the two long bones of the forearm.

Red bone marrow   The tissue that gives rise to blood cells.

Remodeling   The formation of repaired bone after the formation of hard callus.

Respiratory cartilage   The cartilage of the larynx, or voice box, that allows us to generate sound and ultimately speech.

Responsiveness   The ability of muscle cells to react to various stimuli.

Ribs   A series of bones that curve around and protect the chest cavity.

Rickets   A nutritional disorder in which bones weaken and become deformed from too little calcium phosphate.

Sacrum   Five vertebrae just above the coccyx; with age, they fuse and serve as the point of attachment for the hips.

Saddle joint   A biaxial joint at the base of the thumb that allows it to move up and down and toward and away from the fingers.

Sarcolemma   The plasma membrane of a skeletal muscle cell.

Sarcomere   A repeating unit of striated muscle fibrils.

Sarcoplasm   The cytoplasm of a skeletal muscle cell.

Sarcoplasmic reticulum   The endoplasmic reticulum of skeletal muscle cells.

Satellite cell   A muscle cell important in injury repair.

Scaphoid   A boat-shaped bone of the wrist.

Scapula   The triangular flat bone that, along with the collarbone, makes up the pectoral girdle; the shoulder blade.

Serrate sutures   Sutures connected by wavy lines, increasing the total surface of contact, and therefore making the suture strong.

Sesamoid bones   Bones found within tendons that have a rounded end and a more pointed end.

Shaft   The central long portion of a long bone (relative to its longest dimension).

Sharpey's perforating fibers   Little bits of collagen that anchor the periosteum to the surface of bone.

Shivering   Involuntary spasms of skeletal muscles that generate heat.

Short bones   Bones that are approximately the same length in all three dimensions.

Sinuses   Small air-filled pockets within the skull that connect to the respiratory system.

Skeletal muscles   The muscles that allow movement of the body.

Skull   The series of bones that make up the head and jaw.

Smooth muscle   A type of muscle associated with organ tissues that are not under conscious control.

Somatic motor neurons   The nerve cells that stimulate contraction of muscle cells.

Sphincter muscle   A type of muscle that forms a ring and allows constriction of an opening.

Spinal column   *See* Vertebral column.

Spinal cord   The nerve bundle that connects the brain to the rest of the body.

Spongy bone   Bone tissue found in the ends of long bones and in the center of other bones that contains less calcium phosphate than compact bone.

Stem cells   Cells that reproduce rapidly and give rise to multiple types of cells.

Sternum   A flat bone in the front center of the chest that serves for attachment of ribs; the breastbone.

Styloid process   The projection of bone from the radius that is close to the thumb.

Suture   Fibrous joint that closely binds adjacent bones and does not allow the bones to move.

Symphysis   A cartilaginous joint joined by fibrocartilage.

Synarthrosis   A joint that allows very little or no movement; plural, *synarthroses*.

Synchondrosis   A cartilaginous joint joined by hyaline cartilage.

Syndesmosis   A joint where two bones are joined only by a ligament.

Synergist   Muscles in a working group that work additively with the agonist.

Synostosis   A bony joint; plural, *synostoses*.

Synovial fluid   A lubricating, cushioning liquid found in some joints.

Synovial joint   A freely movable joint in which the bones are separated by synovial fluid.

Talus   The bone of the ankle adjacent to the calcaneus.

Tarsal region   The ankle region of the leg.

Tendon   A sheet or strip of tough collagen-containing connective tissue that attaches muscles to bone.

Tendon sheath   A specialized bursa that wraps around a tendon.

Terminal cisternae   In the sarcoplasmic reticulum, small sacs that store calcium ions.

Thoracic vertebrae   The section of vertebrae, usually 12 in number, below the cervical vertebrae, to which the ribs attach.

Tibia   The larger weight-bearing bone of the lower leg.

Trapezium   A near-circular bone of the wrist.

Trapezoid   A four-sided bone of the wrist.

Triquetrum   A triangular bone of the wrist.

Trochlea   The condyle that contacts the ulna.

Trochlear notch   The point of articulation between the humerus and the ulna.

Tropomyosin   The protein found in thin filaments in muscle tissue.

Troponin   A calcium-binding protein in bone.

True ribs   Ribs that connect directly to the sternum through short pieces of cartilage.

Tympanic membrane   The eardrum; a membrane that blocks the entrance to the inner ear and is important in hearing.

Ulna   The larger of the two long bones of the forearm.

Ulnar nerve   The nerve that crosses the medial epicondyle and is the site for stimulation of the "funny bone."

Ulnar notch   The groove in the radius where the ulna contacts the radius.

Unipennate muscles   Feather-shaped muscles where all muscle fibers attach to one side of a tendon.

Vertebra   An irregular bone that helps form the spinal column, or backbone; plural, *vertebrae*.

Vertebral body   *See* Centrum.

Vertebral column   The stacked series of bones of the axial skeleton that surrounds and protects the spinal cord; also called the spinal column or backbone.

Vertebral foramen   The circular opening in each vertebra through which the spinal cord passes.

Vestigial structure   A structure in the body that no longer serves its original purpose and has limited utility.

Voice box   The larynx, a structure involved in sound production and speech.

Volkmann's (perforating) canals   Small canals at right angles to the Haversian canals of the osteon.

Voluntary movement   The movement of a muscle or limb that is under conscious control.

Wrist bones   A cluster of short bones at the junction of the lower arm and hand.

Xiphoid process   A separate, diamond-shaped flat bone at the lower end of the sternum.

Yellow bone marrow   Bone marrow rich in fatty tissue, but containing few, if any, stem cells.

Zone of bone deposition   The site in growing bone where lacunae begin to break down and chondrocytes begin to die off.

Zone of calcification   The site in growing bone where mineralization occurs.

Zone of cell hypertrophy   The growth zone of bone where chondrocytes stop dividing.

Zone of cell proliferation The site toward the center of a bone nearest the zone of reserve cartilage.

Zone of reserve cartilage The region farthest away from the center of the developing bone.

Bibliography

Alcamo, E.I., and B. Krumhardt. *Barron's Anatomy and Physiology the Easy Way.* Hauppauge, N.Y.: Barron's Educational Series, 2004.

Marieb, E.N., J. Mallatt, and P.B. Wilhelm. *Human Anatomy and Physiology.* San Francisco: Benjamin-Cummings Publishing, 2007.

Muscalino, J. *The Muscular System Manual: The Skeletal Muscles of the Human Body.* St. Louis: Elsevier Science Press, 2005.

Saladin, K.S. *Anatomy and Physiology: The Unity of Form and Function.* New York: McGraw Hill Companies, 2006.

Scanlon, V., and T. Sanders. *Essentials of Anatomy and Physiology.* Philadelphia: F.A. Davis Publishing, 2007.

Siegfried, D.E., *Anatomy and Physiology for Dummies.* Hoboken, N.J.: John Wiley and Sons, 2002.

Springhouse, A. *Anatomy and Physiology Made Incredibly Easy.* Springhouse Publishing Company. Philadelphia: Lippincott Williams and Wilkins, 2004.

Stone, R.J., and J.A. Stone. *Atlas of Skeletal Muscles.* New York: McGraw Hill Higher Education, 2008.

Further Resources

Alcamo, E.I. and B. Krumhardt. *Barron's Anatomy and Physiology the Easy Way.* Hauppauge, N.Y.: Barron's Educational Series, 2004.

Anatomy and Physiology Made Incredibly Easy. Springhouse Publishing Company. Philadelphia: Lippincott Williams and Wilkins, 2004.

Aurou, E., and A.M. Tenllado. *Skeletal System.* Broomall, Pa.: Chelsea House Publishers, 1995.

Avila, V. *How Our Muscles Work.* Broomall, Pa.: Chelsea House Publishers, 1994.

MacLeod, J. *Alive: The Living, Breathing Human Body Book.* New York: D.K. Publishing Inc., 2007.

McKinley, M., and V. O'Laughlin. *Human Anatomy.* New York: McGraw Hill Companies, 2007.

Parker, S., and K. Routh. *100 Things You Should Know About the Human Body.* New York: Barnes and Noble, 2004.

Rosen, M.F., and M.C. Oz. *YOU The Owner's Manual: An Insider's Guide to the Body that Will Make You Healthier and Younger.* New York: Collins Publishing, 2008.

Siegfried, D.E., *Anatomy and Physiology for Dummies.* Hoboken, N.J.: John Wiley and Sons, 2002.

Silverstein, A., R. Silverstein, and V.B. Silverstein. *The Muscular System.* Brookfield, Conn.: Millbrook Press, 1995.

Simon, S. *Bones: Our Skeletal System.* New York: HarperCollins Publishing, 2000.

White, K. *Muscular System (Insider's Guide to the Body Series).* New York: Rosen Publishing Group, Inc., 2001.

Web Sites

American College of Sports Medicine, Information on Muscle and Bone Injury
http://www.acsm.org/index.asp

American Orthopaedic Association
http://www.aoassn.org/

Medline Plus, a Service of the National Library of Medicine and the National Institutes of Health
http://www.nlm.nih.gov/medlineplus/medlineplus.html

National Institute of Arthritis and Musculoskeletal and Skin Diseases (NIAMS), National Institutes of Health
http://www.niams.nih.gov/

National Institutes of Health
http://health.nih.gov/

National Osteoporosis Foundation
http://www.nof.org/

Picture Credits

Page

11: (left) Drazen Vukelic/ Shutterstock (right) ayakovlev.com/ Shutterstock
12: © Infobase Publishing
15: Kristin Smith/Shutter-stock
17: © Infobase Publishing
22: © Infobase Publishing
26: © Infobase Publishing
29: © Infobase Publishing
30: © Infobase Publishing
33: © Infobase Publishing
39: © Infobase Publishing
43: © Infobase Publishing
45: © Infobase Publishing
47: © Infobase Publishing
48: © Infobase Publishing
49: © Infobase Publishing
51: © Infobase Publishing
53: © Infobase Publishing
56: © Infobase Publishing
61: © Infobase Publishing
63: © Infobase Publishing

64: © Infobase Publishing
70: © Infobase Publishing
72: © Infobase Publishing
75: Topical Press Agency/ Getty Images
78: © Infobase Publishing
79: © Infobase Publishing
83: (top) Innerspace Imag-ing/Photo Researchers, Inc. (middle) Dr. John D. Cunningham/Visuals Unlimited, Inc. (bottom) Dr. Gladden Willis/Visuals Unlimited, Inc.
86: © Infobase Publishing
89: © Infobase Publishing
91: © Infobase Publishing
93: © Infobase Publishing
98: © Infobase Publishing
99: © Infobase Publishing
101: © Infobase Publishing

Index

About the Author

Dr. Gregory J. Stewart received his Ph.D. in microbiology from the University of California at Davis. His postdoctoral training was conducted at Exxon Research and Engineering and at E.I. DuPont de Nemours and Company. He spent seven years at the University of South Florida as an Assistant and Associate Professor of Biology. In 1993, he joined the Biology Department of the University of West Georgia (then West Georgia College), where he served as Professor and Department Chair for eight years. After a year as Assistant Dean of Arts and Sciences at West Georgia, Dr. Stewart accepted a senior fellowship with the Bureau of Arms Control of the U. S. Department of State. He served as Senior Microbiologist for the Bureau of International Security and Nonproliferation at the State Department. His duties included providing scientific and technical support to the Biological and Toxins Weapons Convention (an international treaty), and serving as an advisor to the Department of State and other U.S. agencies on issues related to microbiology, biological weapons reduction, bioterrorism and counterterrorism threat reduction and response, and biosafety and biosecurity of dangerous pathogenic microorganisms. Dr. Stewart has collaborated with both domestic and international organizations on development of standards for biosafety and pathogen security. He served as a reviewer for the Interagency Select Agent Advisory Group for the National Institutes of Health and for several other national agencies. Dr. Stewart, who is currently a Principal Scientist with Applied Systems Research, Inc., is the author of more than 30 scientific publications. He lives with his wife, Patricia, a clinical microbiologist, and is the stepfather of three grown children and the grandfather of four.